A Slice of
Bill Wundram

A COLLECTION OF 25 YEARS OF COLUMNS
BY THE QUAD-CITY TIMES' BILL WUNDRAM

To BL—
Keep The CHOP's
Strong! Here's To
Carnival of Venice"
and TRIPLE-TONGUING
Make READY FOR
PROF. HULTQUIST and The
FAIR SEASON.

Bill
Wundram
2001

Dedication

To Forrest Kilmer ...

Friend and editor who said one day 25 years ago:
"Wundram, why in the hell
don't you start writing a column?"

Contents

Chapter I

Home Sweet Home

Chapter II

Bill's People

Chapter III

Down the Road

Chapter IV

Clowning Around

Chapter V

Seasonal Musings

Chapter VI

Our Towns

Chapter VII

Worth Repeating

Chapter VIII

Purely Personal

Acknowledgements

IF memory serves me right, this is my 25th year of writing columns. If that means anything — and I doubt that it does — it means lots of words. That is about 9,000 columns, most of the time seven days a week.

I really don't know how you feel about it, dear friends or foes, but it doesn't seem that long. Maybe, if I limp along until 10,000 columns, I will get the hang of it.

How long has it really been? A true story comes to mind of the geezer who inquired at the *Quad-City Times* switchboard if that guy Wundram was still around. When we connected, he said, "Fifty-five years ago, you did a story about how I tripped over my wife's long wedding gown and I fell while going back up the aisle and broke my leg. I wanted to tell you that I don't limp anymore and we're still married."

I was a reporter then, a callow innocent, and that phone call was hard evidence of having spent most of my life around the Times and its predecessors. News has always been like catnip to me, and I have had a love — for as long as I can recall — its tragi-comedy theater, the newsroom.

I seldom look back over past columns, and when I do, it is often embarrassing. A day later, I never like what I wrote the day before. Still, it was suggested that I offer a few slices of some past columns and assemble them into this book. Some of it sounds like it was written by a stranger, because I change. Truly, none of us do things the way we did five years ago or 10 years ago or 25 years ago. We're all naive to think we don't change, because we do, and must face it, even with words.

Change or not, mad or mellowing, maybe some distant day — likely at a garage sale — someone will pick up this book and distill some meaning of the way we lived, the people we remembered and loved in the more irreproachable time before and after this old world groaned into a new century.

Occasionally, I run into a contemporary who asks, "What does it take to be a columnist? Where do you get the ideas, every day of the week?" Herb Caen, the late, lamented columnist of the San Francisco Chronicle, used to tell people, "It takes only a certain lack of imagination and a desire not to do much of anything else."

In closing, may I say affectionate thanks to my good wife, Helen, who has tolerated me with patience — the lovely redhead who realized what she was getting into nearly a half-century ago when, on our first date, I excused myself to go out and cover a fire. She tagged along, and has been at my side for lo, all these years.

May I acknowledge, too, all you people who have been reading me, and writing me, and calling me, and suggesting what I should or shouldn't write about. I think of you as family.

Too, may I acknowledge the keen eye and mind of Deb Brasier, who has been my editor for my most recent books (this, my sixth). I thank the skills of Greg Swanson for designing this book, and for the down-home cover by Ken Prestley. All are good friends.

And by the way, just in case anyone asks, some day I intend to write The Perfect Column. So far, I haven't even come close.

❧

Home Sweet Home

HOME is where the clock ticks and the dog barks and where the milk man used to put the bottles on the back porch.

It was good to come home after school. Home was to smell supper's Swiss steak bubbling on the kitchen stove and, after homework, to play Monopoly on the kitchen table.

Home was a front porch with a swing and little girls playing hopscotch and boys playing ball in the alley.

Home is the place where family bonds are formed.

Home has changed, and I am saddened to observe that. Sometimes, I think home is becoming obsolete because no one is ever there. Parents are chasing the dollars to maintain their homes and chasing around to soccer games and the mall.

Of course, homes — ultimately — are the people who live in them.

I worry about families who have no kitchen table

In this skitter of life, when there is barely/rarely time for the family to flock together for a meal, I think of my mother's kitchen table.

Today, life revolves around the family room, an oblong box-like retreat where one can get buried in the telly or stare out sliding glass doors onto the redwood deck. These are the homes where the kitchen is an afterthought, tucked at one end of that family room with a counter and uncomfortable stools to discourage family dining-conversation.

There may not even be a kitchen table, so I trust memories of my mother's kitchen table.

My mother's kitchen table was big and square, four steps away from the Roper gas stove. My mother's kitchen table bundled our family life into a compact package. Days began and ended at life's epicenter, the kitchen table.

Christmas presents were wrapped there; games were played there; little babies were bundled into their snow suits on my mother's kitchen table; my mother rolled out homemade noodles and scrubbed new potatoes on the kitchen table.

If the rest of the world became detached, one could always depend on my mother's kitchen table as a fragrant, steaming, center of warmth and conversation. On the stove, coffee would be perking 18 hours a day for grownups ... family or neighbors or the milk man. Often, a freshly baked apple pie cooled at its center. If not, cinnamon toast might be gilding under the broiler. We never had a toaster.

It was the table itself, though, that we loved, and where we lived, ate, worried and played. It is unmatched on the diskette of my memory, and I have a notion that family life began going to hell when mom, dad and the kids gave up on the good old kitchen table.

The top of my mother's kitchen table was always covered with flowered oil-cloth, a commodity I daresay doesn't exist anymore. The table — morning, noon and night — had its own network of centerpieces, never to be removed at any season. There was the sugar bowl, the salt and pepper shakers, the bottle of ketchup, the German mustard jar, the cruet of vinegar, the half-open can of Pet milk, the butter crock, and the spooner, a glass utensil that held a dozen teaspoons upright. There was a bowl of oranges, too, to remind of sunshine.

When our family was not eating at the table, talking over the day's joys and sorrows, my two sisters and I would wrangle for a corner of the table, or together the three of us would play games. Always, it was at the kitchen table.

For some reason, food made us think about playing cards, and the two ideas didn't mix — or rather, mixed all too well. When the Old Maid cards got too sticky in a shuffle, after we had stuffed ourselves on slabs of warm bread lathered with grape jelly, we went to something else, like Lotto.

We did our homework at my mother's kitchen table. I built strange, spider-like Erector set doodads on the kitchen table, across from my dad who would be fiddling with grocery store inventories or calculating why he did not make more money on that particular day. My sisters sewed doll clothes or played paper dolls. Once, heaven forbid, I even studied lessons in a course I took from the Northwestern School of Taxidermy.

At night, when my dad had cronies over for home brew, they played euchre at the kitchen table.

Moments after my dad died, the minister gathered with us for prayers and sympathy and coffee at my mother's kitchen table.

The kitchen table was more fragile than we knew at the time. It was something, we felt assured, that always would be in every home. Mother's kitchen table was the bond that held the family together. It was our audience for life.

I worry about families today who grow up without a mother's kitchen table.

è♣

Mom's pantry:
Her palace by the kitchen

What's a pantry, you ask? Few new houses have pantries. But go back a couple generations when almost all houses were designed by men. Our big old home was like that. Men designers thought of only a few things — a place to eat, and a bedroom to sleep, and a room with a couch for dad to take a nap on.

That meant the kitchen was big. It held a sink, a stove, a big table and an ice box. The kitchen did not have a single cupboard, not even the suggestion of a shelf or a counter.

That's where the pantry made its entry. Pantries were wonderful little rooms off the kitchen. They had a door and were never heated.

My mother was obsessed with two things, her kitchen and her pantry. I still can smell the sweet essence of my mother's pantry, with a door that always stuck. A double-sided Sunkist wooden orange crate on the left was storage for potatoes, carrots, rutabagas and other stuff from the ground. Above that crate and on both sides were shelves to the ceiling for dishes and pots and pans and kitchen towels and canned goods and the company china.

I think that now, 60 years later, I could walk into my mother's shadowy old pantry, and on the left-hand side on the floor, I could reach into a wooden apple crate and instantly find a hammer, screwdriver, a couple flat tins of Shinola shoe polish and a new set of shoestrings.

There was some fig of imagination that things kept fresher in the pantry.

The cakes and pies were always put there to cool after coming out of the oven. The pantry door, always closed, was supposed to keep bread pudding fresher than any place in the kitchen.

When spring cleaning began, my mom would take every single thing out of the pantry, scrub the shelves and then put down new shelf paper with frilly edges. Doing that, I am sure, gave her a great deal of satisfaction.

On the second pantry shelf, low enough for the kids to reach, was the tin bread box, a receptacle for the Peter Pan bread, which was a dime a loaf, and the round carton-boxes of Quaker Oats. Everyone had to have oatmeal for breakfast, because it would stick to your ribs. I can still hear my mother insisting that "Oatmeal sticks to your ribs."

My mother's pantry held everything, because you must remember that the kitchen had no cabinets or storage places. The pantry had a flour bin, and pickles in a crock, and half a shelf of homemade grape jelly with paraffin lids.

The corner for the syrup was always sticky, because the blue-label Karo came in gallon tin pails. I suppose one could say that the pantry in every home was a little walk-in grocery store.

Our pantry had a tiny window. In the winter, a wooden box was fitted into that window, and the sash closed down on it. It made an efficient refrigerator that would even set Jell-O. In the summer, although I don't care to get into that misery, we had a wooden ice box regularly serviced by the ice man lugging a big cake of ice.

As time went by, my mother had cabinets mounted in her kitchen. But still her pantry was always full. The cut glassware, the goblets and "company" china had an ordained place on the top shelf.

Unto her dying day, at age 93, my mother remembered and loved her pantry.

She had been in a nursing home several years, and her gray old head was getting hazy. One day, she complained about a fly in her room and ordered me:

"Go fetch the fly swatter. It's hanging on the pantry door, under the calendar."

ᐓ

Table prayers —
from grace to grapes

Table graces bring a family close together. They keep us in close touch with God and help to remember those in need. Many people link hands as a physical symbol of the link between family and friends and those at the table as all of God's children on earth.

I've been collecting table graces for years, and find that most are serious and thankful, but some have a twinkling wit. God might appreciate the latter. I choose to think he enjoys a good laugh.

That reminds of a Sunday when we brunched at a restaurant with a friend, the Rev. Al VanderMeer. The food was brought and Preacher Al, the lofty Midwest synod exec for the Reformed Churches in America, chose to say a few words over the food.

"We want to say grace," Al interrupted the chatty waitperson. She paid no heed, but quickly reached for a plate of fruit. We folded hands and bowed heads.

"Oh," she abruptly said. "Grace? I thought you wanted grapes."

Grace or grapes, here are some of my favorite graces, harvested from hither and there, many gathered by Paul Simpson McElroy, a contemporary religious thinker, and from the little book, "Table Graces, Prayers of Thanks," and table graces I have heard, particularly at Thanksgiving.

> *Give me a good digestion, Lord,*
> *And also something to digest.*
> *Give me a healthy body, Lord,*
> *With sense to keep it at its best.*
> *— Found in old Chester Cathedral, England*

Accept, O Father, our humble thanks for this our daily bread;
and as it adds strength to our mortal bodies,
may it give us power to render better service to Thee.
— An old Methodist prayer of grace

On this Thanksgiving, O God, what brightens the eye?
What brings out the best in us is the rich pumpkin pie.
— John Greenleaf Whittier

Once more we come, Lord, to this day of special Thanksgiving. Our thoughts are turned to the past year. The days have rolled into the seasons, the seasons into the year. Each day has been crowded with Thee. Each season has brought new proofs of Thy loving forethought. May we this Thanksgiving day pledge our gratitude anew. Continue, we pray Thee, to surround us with Thy care.
— A prayer from the Amish in Kalona, Iowa

God, make us able
For all that's on the table. Amen.
— Eire

As we join hands, let us come together, rich and poor, black and white, young and old, enjoying each other's uniqueness. Just as each season brings a new loveliness, so does each man and woman bring forth a special gift, making this world a more beautiful place to live in. Amen.
— A Presbyterian prayer of grace

Give us Lord, a bit o' sun,
A bit o' work and a bit o' fun;
Give us all in the struggle and sputter
Our daily bread and a bit o' butter.
— On the wall of an inn, Lancaster, England

The kitchen drawer
that we all love best

I love that little junk drawer in our kitchen. It contains everything I never need. Every kitchen I have ever known has had a junk drawer. Now, we have remodeled, removing a booth that I never fitted into, and a useless island. Now that we have added a counter with more drawers, my wife insists that a junk drawer would be out of place among shiny oak cabinets.

A household could exist without a living room, because no one ever uses the living room. But a household could not exist without a junk drawer.

I inventoried our old junk drawer the other day and there was not a single item I could part with. I would suppose that its contents were like those found in the junk drawers of most every kitchen. How could anyone part with these items, much less survive without them?

In our junk drawer, the contents of which have been transported from several homes we have occupied, I counted 18 keys, none of which fit anything around the house. Also, two locked padlocks. None of the keys fit them. I found 14 ballpoint pens (none of which worked) about 200 rubber bands, a like number of paper clips and a two-year-old phone book. A person couldn't part with that phone book because it has all kinds of important numbers scribbled on the cover and on the inside page.

There were any number of important wire twisties, a handful of spring clothespins (some in separate pieces) and a flashlight without a bulb. Some day I will get a bulb for it, and it will be handy if the lights go out some night. There also were eight batteries of different sizes. I don't know if they work or not, but they should be saved just in case they do. Oh, and I cannot overlook the three stubs of candles that had seen much better days.

There were two extension cords and more odd-shaped screws and nails than

I cared to count. The nails were little ones, left over from putting up curtain rods two houses ago. I found half a pair of pliers, important to be saved because some day I may find the other half.

There was a lot of loose string, a hardened paint brush, Matchbox cars from the kids who are now grown people, fuses (handy to have around though we are in a circuit-breaker house that doesn't need fuses), a Phillips screwdriver with the working end so worn that it is handy to use as an ice pick, a package of morning glory seeds that I am going to plant come springtime, and the registration for a car that I no longer own.

Never to be parted with were two expired metal license tags that I never put on the collar of Polly, our dear, long-dead dog, a little plastic bottle of dried-up Elmer's Glue, a hammer that was quite useless because it had no handle (but some day I shall get one) and a sheet of fourth-grade photos of one of our kids. The sheet had about two dozen of the same picture of the child, to be cut out and distributed among aunts and uncles and grandparents. I never got around to cutting them out, but I must save that precious sheet of photographs of Becky.

The marvel of a junk drawer is that with one hand you can reach in and lift everything out in one hunk. It all seems to tangle together, as if destined to be forever joined.

"You've just got to get rid of that stuff," my wife insisted.

Reluctantly, I made an effort. The only thing I could toss out was a sheet of coupons, good for $1 off on medium-size Happy Joe's pizzas. Shucks, they had expired in 1999.

❧

Saving a pal that's a 'slice' of our life

It's turned bread into 71,540 pieces of morning toast; we couldn't give it up

There is affection for any item that is a familiar friend, no matter what its age or condition.

Most sentimental people have an affection for everything. I can't throw away an old necktie that I haven't worn for six years. I can't part with an old pair of shoes because someday I might need an old pair of shoes to wear outside in the mud to trim some bushes. I can't toss out an old pair of pants because you never know when you might need an old pair of pants if you're going to paint something.

As for my wife, she cannot throw away a box or a bow or any faded snapshot or any skirt or dress that no longer fits. In truth, she can't throw away anything!

So, when our beloved pop-up toaster conked out, we couldn't part with it. It looked like new, shiny chrome plate with streamline rounded sides and ends, Bakelite handles, a control knob for browning and a removable crumb tray.

It had toasted our tears and triumphs for 49 years of marriage. It toasted the Wonder bread for me in mornings when I was more morning sick than my wife during three pregnancies. That 1952 Toastmaster browned the first nibbles of toast for the little teeth of our three babies; it provided at least 10,000 BLT sandwiches in 49 years of unfailing service; it was the fixture for 1,001 late-night treats, basted with cinnamon and sugar. That grand, shiny old toaster *was* our lives.

When it quit, I was ready to weep. It was a wedding gift from Henry Hook, good old "Hollerin' Hank," then publisher of the Davenport Democrat. He was so gratified that I had settled down that the day after our wedding, he also gifted us with a giant Mixmaster. Only the green bowls remain after lo, all these years. The Mixmaster gave out long ago.

But the toaster steadily toasted, on and on and on ... until the other day.

No amount of poking could make it work again. Its day had come. Facetiously, I figured that in 49 years it had faithfully toasted 71,540 pieces of morning toast, and only God himself knows how many slices of bread it had browned for peanut butter snacks. Nothing can last forever, I reasoned, but in desperation took it to K & K Hardware in Bettendorf. They can fix anything. Still, the repairman looked at it and shook his head.

"This is an antique. Look at that cord. It's a fabric wrap." He was skeptical if it was worth the effort, if even possible, to repair.

In the end, all it needed was a new cord, and now it is toasting merrily away and our kitchen and ourselves are happy again.

Still, that business of it being an antique piqued my interest. I searched out "A Collectors Guide to Toasters & Accessories" (Helen Greguire, 150 pages, Collector Books). That book told me the first toasters were contraptions carefully placed on the gas stove for the low flames to toast the bread. Not until 1906 was the first electric toaster patented, and this book showed that some fancy old electric toasters could be worth up to $3,500.

And there, in the book I spotted our beloved Toastmaster, a color photo in all its shining glory. Should it be worth $500, I'd sell it to anyone. Sentimentality could end in a hurry. But the fine print showed it wasn't worth much more than $30 today, hardly more than what it cost to begin with.

So, there it shall remain in our kitchen, hopefully toasting forever. It has only a single fault. The slots are not wide enough to accommodate English muffins. But then, when we got it in 1952, no one had heard of English muffins in the Quad-Cities.

ଽଌ

Living rooms
are good for what?

This afternoon, I plan to drop into our living room and take a nap. It will be the first time I have spent any time there since we took down the Christmas tree.

We really have a nice living room, but nobody sits in there. It makes me try to figure out if living rooms are really good for anything.

On a glass-topped coffee table there is a story from the New York Times questioning the use and the future of the living room. I agree with the story. The living room of today is useless.

Too bad. Our living room is the nicest room in our condo. It is a big room, sort of an L-shaped thing with one nook for the dining room set. But mostly, it is a living room. There are, if you count the four dining room chairs, 14 places to sit. But no one ever sits there except when we have company, which isn't very often.

I keep thinking this room must really be so lonely. Oh, I walk through it to turn the heat up or down and I admire the view from the big picture window.

It has draw drapes and a lovely view. It looks out on nice lawns, and in summer, I can glance out that big window onto my neighbors' deck and see what they are cooking for dinner on the grill.

But still, we never sit in our living room. "Maybe we should clean the rug," my wife said. No one ever uses the rug, but we just had it cleaned anyway, and it looks the same creamy-white as it did before.

"We need more color in our living room," my wife said. So we bought a big, splashing painting of California poppies by Davenport's Sarah Metz Wood. It adds a lot of life to the room, and I fondly admire it from the kitchen. But still, we do not sit in the living room. "I think I'll have Sarah paint us some pussy willows to go by the poppies," my wife said. "That wall needs pussy willows," as if that is the answer.

Maybe it's because we don't have a telephone in our living room. "But you're always on the phone, and you'd spill your diet pop all over the rug," my wife protested. So we don't have a telephone in the living room.

Also, we don't have a TV set in the living room. If we did, I would be stretched out on the couch, watching "20/20" and falling asleep before the news comes on, spilling my diet pop.

I wondered if the lighting was wrong, so the other day — when they had a sale — I went to the store and spent a fortune on track lights. I don't know if they will help any more than the pussy willows.

Frankly, I don't have the hint of a clue as to what to do about our living room. I feel so sorry for it, with no one ever there to share its matching blue chairs.

I keep thinking that someday we are going to use that living room, but my wife likes it just the way it is. She says it is the only room in the house that stays clean.

કેરી

For the love of a house ...

There is a thing called "house karma." Houses have a soul, just as much as a ship (or, for that matter, a newspaper).

I'm lucky. I have always lived in a house, albeit sometimes a condo. But never an apartment. Houses have special karma.

A house is like a friend. It embraces you and hugs you every time you enter its doors. It wants to say, "Hi, you're home again. Here I am, waiting for you!"

I get choked up about houses. Sometimes when I see a little kid, I think of houses and our own kids and the big place where they grew up.

I even think furniture has karma, like the wingback chair we bought second-hand, and sat in to bottle-feed all three of our babies. I would get up for the 3 a.m. feeding, holding Peter in that big chair, and both of us would fall asleep. I wish we had kept that chair.

That is why I am so sentimental about houses, because all houses we have lived in have had good house karma.

Our houses all carried personalities; they shared our joy and comforted in the most tragic of times. So distinctly, I remember walking into the first house we ever owned. It had a fireplace and big corner windows, and — wonder of wonders — Venetian blinds. Impulsively, I told the real estate man, "I'll take it." Never mind that my wife-to-be, who was in an out-of-town nursing residency, had not seen it.

That house was so tiny that it didn't need much furniture. Good thing, because we were so poor we couldn't even afford decorations for our first Christmas tree. We used bows from wedding gifts as ornaments. But that first house, with a shoebox-size kitchen, had a loving karma.

We had been there but two brief years when a wise banker wanted to buy it.

Why would a wealthy banker want a tiny house like this, we wondered, but he offered $18,500. A fortune! How could I make money any quicker? Little did an oaf like me imagine that our house soon would be the site of a shopping mall.

We moved into our grandest house of all, with pillars, the dream of my wife, who walked by it as a teen when it was being built and hoped she would some-day live there. *That* was a house with karma, a bit haunted around the edges, but a house that refined with age and grew in karma.

Always, we knew this big house was our place, and sometimes I wonder why we left, but we did. It was late on a snowy night when Pete and I finally cleaned the last trifling junk from the attic. I scribbled a note to the new owners: "Steve and Krista, may this home offer you the joy it gave us for 25 years." It did. Steve and Krista stayed for 18 years. The house had karma for them, too.

We tried the bluffs of Pleasant Valley for a few years, struggling with two acres of hillsides and apple trees and a defiant house that was an architect's dream and, too often, a homeowner's despair. With a stone floor and an atrium with jas-mine, it had unprecedented karma.

When we moved on, the buyers said, "This is *the* place," and they are still there, with enough karma to last forever.

At first, condo life was for us. Building a fireplace in the kitchen brought a cozy karma, but watching golfers waste their time was not my bag, so we opted again for a house — 4,400 feet of rambling space on a woodsy hillside, a serene neighborhood with deer nibbling the lawn and the karma of having entertained the whole Chicago White Sox ball club and forgotten movie stars the likes Alice Faye and band leader Phil Harris. Nine rooms were too much, though, and we sold. But on our last day there, we stood alone and cried together in the new sunporch. Farewell to karma.

All houses have karma, and we have found new karma in a 3,000-square-foot condo. A skylight spews cold, and the aluminum siding creaks at night in zero weather, but such things are just part of the personality of a house.

Now, I snuggle into a wingback chair again, watching the fire, but with no babies to feed.

All houses have karma. Someday, we may test the karma of another.

I have always wanted to live in a lighthouse.

ঽঌ

Life is poorer
without an alley to play in

There are any number of reasons why kids go wrong, but let's assume that it's because they don't build alleys anymore.

Even developers and real estate people lament their loss, but it's always the bottom line, y'know. Alleys gobble space where other homes could be built.

When was the last time you saw a Quad-City subdivision built with an alley? The houses can be $350,000 or $500,000 with $4,000 a month payments and $900 utility bills.

But no alleys!

The old alley where we kicked the can and played scrubs has been bottled up in the builders' time capsule. The alley is gone, the place where parents could always keep an eye on their kids. Not just little kids, but teens loved alleys.

We didn't need playgrounds or such things to amuse us when we had the alley.

Even in winter, the alley — one with a slope — was the slickest place for sledding. Alleys were never scraped by plows, and had little traffic.

An alley was the best of all places in early springtime to play basketball, using the hoop on some cooperative neighbor's garage, or to learn to ride a two-wheeler. It was safe, too, usually devoid of vehicles except for the milkman driving through, or someone backing out of a garage.

A manhole cover was always baseball's home plate, and woe be to the miscreant who smacked the ball into some ornery neighbor's yard or onto a flat garage roof. No more ball game today, kids.

And always, the official alley flower was the hollyhock.

Attached garages are what killed the alley. Everyone used to have a garage out back by the alley. Where else where you supposed to put your car? You washed your car by the garage in the alley, usually with a bucket of water and a chamois.

. And anyone who did not put his car in the garage every night invited gossip.

Neighbors clucked if you left it out front of the house for more than a half-day.

At any time of day, no matter where you lived, you could find kids playing in the alley — even in the winter. Alleys seemed to slip into obscurity at 5 p.m., when everyone went in for supper, but they came to life again near dark when hide and seek was the pleasure. Then the street lights would softly flicker on. Everyone knew it was time to head for home when the street lights came on. On the way, you'd catch a few lightning bugs.

Sure, there are alleys left, so long as there are old neighborhoods around, but some day, for certain, there will be no more alleys. They will disappear from the language.

"It's sad. I love alleys; I grew up in Oelwein, Iowa, and we always played in the alley," Rob Fick, president of Mel Foster Co., once told me. Fick agrees that the attached garage helped make the alley obsolete. We became too lazy to walk across the back yard from the alley to the house. The garage had to be attached.

The garage, too, become a product of the grid system of subdivisions. Long ago, neighborhoods were platted in a grid system of squares and rectangles.

Now, it's cul-de-sacs.

The advent of underground utilities brought an end to alleys, too. Power poles all were in the alley. As it turned out, there was the little thing called "expense." Alleys devoured land, and no present-day developer is ready to surrender an extra few lots in a subdivision for the paving of an alley.

All of this spells "suburbia," and that means you put the garbage cans out by the front curb every Monday morning instead of leaving them back by the alley where they belong.

Well, we are always panting to embrace progress, and so I suppose the loss of the alley is the way that things must be.

Still, when I drive through new subdivisions, I sense that something is wrong. An alley offered elbow room between our present tightly pressed new houses. And too, we forfeited neighborliness. The man next door, when he put his car into the garage by the alley, called out into the dusk to his neighbors: "Good night, folks."

ɞ🌢

Home is obsolete:
No one's ever there

If you spend a lot of time on the telephone, as I do, you find that most of the time nobody's home to answer your call.

Where is everybody? Are they out there, drifting in some metaphysical aura, wafting in outer space?

Everyone has to be someplace, but they are not at home. Why do they even own a home? Why do they own a living room with a nice soft sofa? Obviously, they don't sit on it because they never are at home.

Pick out a dozen random telephone numbers in the Quad-Cities. Call them, and no one will be home. If you do get an answer, it probably will be one of those loathsome answering machines. A voice will say, "I'm sorry, but we can't come to the phone right now. If you will leave your name and number at the sound of the beep, we will get back to you as soon as possible..."

Beep!

Well, I don't exactly like answering machines (nor does any sensible person), but have come to rely on them at home and office. The world is full of answering machines. Everyone has one.

I called a Quad-City company that sells answering machines and got — what else? — an answering machine: "We are out of the office at this time ... blah, blah, blah, blah."

At another place that sells such devilish devices, a sales rep said that 75 percent of the homes in America now have answering machines. Also, some people use the machine as a mere excuse for not answering the phone.

"They monitor calls," this person said. "They are at home and call back only those people they wish to talk to."

Telephone companies say they don't sell nearly as many teen lines as they used to because kids are not at home as much anymore.

But back to the question of where is everyone? If people are not at home, where are they? Have they disappeared into some big black hole in space, the place where most politicians should go?

What about the poor Avon Lady or the Fuller Brush Man. Do they ever find anyone home? Avon Co. says, "You just don't knock on the door anymore because no one will be home." At the Tupperware district office in Davenport, the boss said, "You don't find people home very often. Our representatives call and make arrangements for a visit or contact. The majority of our calls are at night, because everyone in the household is working. It's not easy to find people at home."

If the city-fied people are not at home, country folks certainly must still be. But no one is home down on the farm either to answer the phone. Dad is out tending the stock, or working in town, and mom is doing the same.

Once, I was lost in the country north of DeWitt, Iowa, and must have driven into a dozen farmyards to ask directions. I was met by yapping dogs but no one to answer the door.

In other words (as if there are any) absolutely nobody is ever home. For three days, I have been trying to contact a particular woman.

"Oh, have you been on vacation?" I asked her.

"No, it's just that we are never home. The kids have basketball practice after school, and then I have been working on a hospital event and fun night at school has taken a lot of time. I'm never home."

The world has lapsed into absentia. No one is ever home.

Home is obsolete.

ૐ

Home: A little word that fills a column

I like to hear stories of home.

Whenever I ask someone of age about home, they show snapshots. Grandmas will purse their lips and pull out snaps of kids around Christmas trees or blowing out birthday candles. But always, it is at home.

That is how it should be — a reassurance there is a place we all know thoroughly: Home.

Always, my memories are of home, some home where I have lived, and came to know with heart and soul. Make no mistake, the American Dream begins at home.

A lifetime ago, I left the old family home, the west end Davenport place I grew up in ... a double lot with peonies and apple trees and a goldfish pond. Funny, but you never forget home.

I remember there were 14 steps to reach our second floor, and that I always slept in what my sisters called "the cold room." For some reason, the hot air registers from our old octopus-pipe coal furnace never were connected to my room.

There is another new owner at that west end home. She sent me a snapshot of the old home place, wondering about that "cold room" and hoped that her years would be as happy as those I spent in the big old house with the white fence at West 5th and Oak.

I still like to drive along our old street, remembering the Walcher's Bakery man who rang a hand bell from his truck for those who wanted fresh bread (in a paper sack), cream horns or jelly doughnuts called by the Teutonic name of berliners.

Memories never erase. I knew thoroughly the terraced roots of the walnut tree by our back porch, and at night would scare my sleeping sisters when walnuts thumped on the roof. I would shout, "burglars, burglars." That tree is still there, 70 years later.

Odd, isn't it, how one recalls trifles of that childhood home — like those 14 steps to the second floor — when today you can't even remember to bring home a loaf of bread. Gosh, I could call our first real-operator phone number today, if needed — Walnut 1661.

Home was always a flurry of neighborhood kids sliding down our cellar door and getting splinters in their bottoms, and a playhouse for my sisters, and the chocolate-colored mohair couch in the parlor where you were allowed to settle down and read a big-little book about Flash Gordon.

Every home has a story of warmth, roots, anchors, origins, cradles and conception, tension and tears. I was born in the old home place, rather unexpectedly in the dining room. In an upstairs bedroom, my father died.

The quality of our life was more important than our standard of living, though I remember we lived middle-average lives. The doorstep was the center of our existence, where neighborhood kids stood to yell, "Billy or Ruthie or Helen, can you come out to play?" Kids never knocked or rang doorbells long ago, they just stood outside and yelled your name. That sounds strange, today.

A thousand children have thundered up and down those west end sidewalks since I left, and I once found it difficult to return to the home place for just a single visit. The front door was the same; it still stuck. But like my life, everything was different.

After marriage, we settled into a big, rambling place where we lived so happily for a couple dozen years, rearing kids and beginning chapters anew of stories of home with a family of our own. That pillared place on Bettendorf's River Drive had a plethora of neighborhood kids, and after supper time, one of our own would put up a sign, "Yard Games Tonight," on the back fence. Until summer's darkness, our back yard was a shouting, circular field of motion. The pitcher's mound for kickball was always churned to the bare earth, and I despaired during all of our years there, if grass would ever grow again.

I drove through our family's old Bettendorf alley the other day. I paused to look. There have been two owners since we left, and lo, after all these years, grass has grown on the pitcher's mound.

ॐ

Bill's People

PEOPLE come into our lives and they go out again. Most of them I cannot forget. They have impressed me, made me laugh and cry, and they have taught me.

Often, they have humbled me.

Big people make the headlines, but I have found the little people most fascinating. I usually steer away from those with their noses in the air and write about people like Grandma, who spent a happy decade of days on a mall bench, or the friendly old Swede who pedaled his bike to Davenport every day across the Government Bridge.

I like to subscribe to Abe Lincoln, who said, "The Lord prefers common people. That is the reason he makes so many of them."

In the simple, slow lane with Henning ...

Good old Henning Gotthard Olson. He was as warm and sweet as hot buttered rum.

"That's funny," they used to muse about Henning, the thin, quiet Rock Island man who pumped his balloon-tired bike across the Government Bridge every day that it was open.

Life cruises slowly for commonplace people like Henning Gotthard Olson, age 88. The Quad-City world is full of such people, and when they die, there are precious few left behind to mourn. They depart this weary old world, leaving little except meek memories.

Some people live extravagant, floppy-disc lives with flashy cars and big homes. That's the way to do it today.

Henning Gotthard Olson was from the "old school" — a cliche that most of us never quite understood — but Henning used to quietly say that he was from the "old school."

Henning Olson lived his life in very small doses.

So far as anyone knows, he never had a car. He never had a wife. He lived in the same room most of his life, outliving three landlords. If to be simple is to be great, then Henning Olson should have won an Oscar and an Emmy and a few Golden Globes.

After Henning's death, a great-nephew picked up his belongings.

"It hardly took an hour to clear out his tidy room," he said. "It would take a truck to gather the average person's accumulation. Not Uncle Henning. All the neckties he ever owned were on one wire coat hanger."

He owned two suits, a summer suit and a winter suit. He was put to rest in his neat brown double-breasted suit. Among the folded effects in a dresser drawer were clippings from newspapers proclaiming his prowess as the checker champion of Davenport's LeClaire Park. That's where he would ride his old balloon-tired Schwinn bike every summer day, to play checkers. After a few dozen years, he out-lived all his partners.

He would ride his bike to church, too. When the pastor of First Lutheran in Rock Island first came to the church, he wondered who was the little fellow push-ing his old bike up the hill to attend Sunday services. That was Henning, all right. In the summer, he always wore a straw hat. Sometimes, in the chill weather, too.

As might be expected of one from the "old school," Henning was from the "old country" — Sweden. He came first to the farm, drawn by the black prairie soil that ran in a belt across country and towns like Bishop Hill, Galva, Galesburg, Swedona and above the rivers in Rock Island and Moline. He left the farm and moved to the cities where he worked in the shops. All the time, he biked everywhere.

He pedaled that old bike all seasons, nodding sweetly to strangers, and partic-ularly the widows who never were able to catch the old Swede.

Several dozen people were at his funeral. Some were from the meal site where he dined at noon. The old women clucked, "He was the politest man who ever lived." His omnipresent straw hat was perched on his casket.

There was a simple burial service at shady Grove Hill Cemetery, Morrison, Ill.

Question, if you wish, why there should be a whole column devoted to a quiet little common man that nobody much knew, and who kept all the neckties he ever owned on one coat hanger.

Well, Lincoln said, "The Lord prefers common people. That is the reason he makes so many of them."

Adlai Stevenson did a pretty good job, too, on quiet, simple common folk.

"In quiet people, there is vision and a purpose. Many things are revealed to the humble that are hidden from the great."

ॐ

The mall is sad, Grandma's dead

When customers began to ask, "Where's Grandma?" a worried stir went through Davenport's NorthPark Mall.

They missed the dear LOL (little old lady) who sat — day in, day out — for at least 25 years on mall benches, throwing kisses, cootchy-cooing babies and being her lovable 90-year-old self.

Yesterday, the mall was sad. There was no counselor for the weary, no one to cluck, "tsk, tsk" to rambunctious teens, no one to offer, "bless you, sir" or "thank you, ma'am" to well-wishers.

Grandma is dead.

Most did not even know her name. Ferne Davis was an anonymity, rather a pleasantly benign mystery. Only a week or so back I had written of her, leaving identity out of the copy. "Shush," she shyly, ever so quietly, whispered to me. "No one needs to know who I am. I'm just here."

She loved the murmur of the Christmas crowds, speaking plans of her own Christmas with a daughter, Frances Keller, Davenport.

But Dec. 20 was her final day on the bench, a quiet oasis in the surge of shoppers. She felt ill, so Frances — with whom she lived — took Grandma to the hospital. She died a few days later. Congestive heart failure, they said.

Some might have wondered about the elderly woman on the mall bench. But it wasn't a matter for concern; she simply wanted to be around people rather than sit home.

"Mom would have it no other way than to spend all her time at the mall. She wouldn't have lived to be 90 — she would have died 20 years earlier — if she hadn't been surrounded by people every day," her daughter says.

"She would fight to get to the mall," a NorthPark representative says. "Her daughter drove her here between 7 and 7:30 a.m. daily, in time to greet the mall walkers. Late in the afternoon, her daughter took her home."

All day Grandma sat, studying the mores and manners of the regulars, the ebb and flow of mall customers. Likely, she was a better barometer of business traffic than any economist. A few times daily she slowly made the rounds, supported by a little shopping cart given by Walgreens when that store closed up in the mall. In the morning, Grandma took over one corner of a bench in front of JC Penney, and by mid-morning would stroll to a bench in front of Younkers. At noon, she bought coffee at McDonald's and a sandwich at Chik-Fil-A. "Always, she insisted on paying," said Lucky Lang, owner of Chik-Fil-A.

After lunch Grandma napped, sitting up, or sometimes in a semi-curl on a mall bench, cozy with a lap robe made for her by Margaret Immesoete, Moline.

Her obituary was 4 inches, but for those who knew Grandma, it might have been for a princess.

"She was the grandest of the grandmas," says Margaret VanFossen, whose sixth-grade students at Williams Intermediate School, Davenport, would send her Christmas cards addressed to the mall.

With Christmas and all, it took a while for word of Grandma's death to reach her friends. The morning mall walkers — with whom Grandma had such rapport — were shocked. Dee Lang, Rock Island, took up an offering from some fellow walkers and collected $51. She says, "Everyone pitched in a dollar except one lad from the food court. He could afford it far less than most of the people, but gave $2. We don't want it for funeral flowers, but something more satisfactory."

Grandma's little shopping cart was kept nightly in the mall office.

Employees eagerly helped her push it up a ramp to her morning "sit" by Penney's. She insisted on helping, so they agreeably said, "We'll push it together."

Grandma's little cart was placed in storage — forever? — because there will never be another Grandma like her at NorthPark. She was one-of-a-kind, a quarter-century institution.

It would be nice if someone saw fit to make a bronze plaque and mount it on one of the benches: A Bench In Memory of Grandma.

On the back of a mall bench ...

One morning, about a week after Ferne Davis was buried, a brass plaque was mounted on Grandma's favorite bench outside Younkers and near Fannie May at NorthPark. That was the spot where she spent most of her days for 25 years. Grandma, a gentle landmark, was one of those mall personalities everyone seemed to know.

Dashawn Pernell, manager of the Marketplace at NorthPark, was one of Grandma's dearest buddies, and was determined that something had to be done in her memory. Merchants who came to know Grandma as a mall fixture asked him, "Do you need anything?" A bronze marker was purchased. Things Remembered handled engraving; the hardware department of Sears pitched in. There was a simple ceremony when the plaque was attached to a bench: In Loving Memory of Ferne Davis — Grandma.

ۿ

'Everyone is significant,
even the custodian'

On a long-ago last day of school, during English lit class at old Davenport High, unforgettable Hortense Finch gave us a pop quiz.

For some reason, probably because I was scared of this precise teacher, I breezed through the questions. So did my old chum, Dick Prose, who was probably the smartest kid in the class.

Then we came to the last question: "What is the first name of the custodian who cleans the halls and rooms on this floor?" I smiled and kept on writing.

Dick whispered, "This must be some kind of joke," and handed in the test, leaving the last question blank. He asked the teacher if that question about the custodian would count toward our quiz grade.

"Of course," Miss Finch said sternly. "In your lives ahead, you will meet many people. Everyone is significant, even the custodian. All people deserve your attention and care, even if all you do is smile and say hello."

Dick said he never forgot that lesson. He also learned that the custodian's name was Max.

I told him that the fellow's full name was Max Detlefs. Kids never paid much attention to the friendly man pushing the broom, but he and I became good friends. We joshed and sometimes shared Milky Way candy bars. I remember Max better than I do most of my teachers. He was bald and shocked the whole school when I once brought him a fright wig, which he wore for a full day.

I've never forgotten that lesson about everyone being significant, even the custodian in a hall of academia.

⨪

There's always hope ... Bob Hope

It's not every sunny afternoon that you climb into the front seat of a limo and make chit-chat with the couple in the back seat.

He's not sure who I am; I just say that I'm Bill. The couple just happens to be Bob and Dolores Hope.

No questions asked.

He perches at the edge of the seat, still that indefinable ski nose, a mere 87 on this afternoon, hardly looking old enough for Social Security. He's wise-cracking, cruising in a big white limousine from Quad-City International Airport to Davenport, where he has a performance that night.

He looks at the Mississippi River and snaps: "That's where you have all the gambling boats. Is Pete Rose dealing blackjack?"

He spies downtown Davenport: "It's going to be a nice city if it ever gets finished."

Hope's a little hard of hearing, a cup of hand to the ear, but ever the comic on this never-never-land ride, like I'm on the "Road to Morocco" with Dottie Lamour. But this time, Bob is with his wife, Dolores. He pats her hand and she grabs his: "I'm getting too old to stay home alone, so we do a lot of shows together."

Hope makes a dirty look at the mention of "old."

He is in tennies and a white billed cap with Mickey Mouse on the front. He and Dolores hustled aboard their $3 million, four-engine blue-bellied Jet Star at mid-morning in Burbank, Calif., for a quick flight to the Quad-Cities where Bob is doing a show that night. He didn't have a chance to shave, but not even his whiskers are gray.

Bob Hope, the classic, of the genre of Red Skelton, one of his hero compatriots. Sure, Hope's old, but makes a little soft shoe shuffle on the floor of the limo and jokes about "that creaky old geezer, George Burns."

I ask, "Don't you ever get tired?" He tugs on that white Mickey Mouse cap and groans: "Well, I do sleep a lot. I sleep during my shows."

Hope looked a little faded, stooping as he climbed down the stairs of his personal plane at the airport. But when he spotted TV cameras and the newsies, he brightened upright — curtain call — and he was on an imaginary stage, a little jog, a quip. Someone should have been playing, "Thanks for the memories."

"I've been here before, in the Quad-Cities when Ed McMahon gave his name to a golf tournament here. And then they gave me an honorary degree from a college — St. Ambrose. Now I get my education watching 'Jeopardy.' I'm so dumb I have to tape it, and run it back at half speed so I can get the answers."

Bob turns to admire the Mississippi along River Drive, and one appreciates — at close range — that unique Hope profile, a droop-snoop ski-run. Monarchs like England's King George VI have made jest of it.

Dolores, who sings with his show (standards like "Just the Way You Are,") does a lot of the talking. Bob smiles and listens. Wifely, she says that he has a cold. Husbandly, he corrects, "I'm getting over a cold." He's ready to sneeze, quickly rolls down the limo window, and achoos into the air, but so quick with the gibe. He tells Dolores: "I checked first to see if the wind was in the right direction."

We gab and chat, like talking to the people across the street. I tell Dolores: "For some strange reason, my wife and I are on your Christmas card list. I'll never know why two unknowns get a pretty card from you every year, but there is one mystery. The Christmas card, year in, year out, never comes until the middle of January." She points a finger at Bob, "That's because he never gets around to mailing them." He blushes.

Thanks for the memories.

❧

A brick-and-mortar tribute to love eternal

Visitors who pass by the strange little brick house in the middle of Davenport's Oakdale Memorial Park always wonder, the same as I, what and who and why.

Visitors regularly stop at the cemetery office, puzzled to find a tiny house — actually the size of a child's playhouse with porch and fireplace — among the more traditional burial markers.

One can envision Robert Nott, respected citizen of Davenport, personally mortaring the bricks into place 88 years ago for the little house in Oakdale.

No other person would be capable of doing the work, for this would be where he and his wife, Anna, would spend eternity together. Nott was hurrying the project, for life was passing swiftly for Anna. She would be dead by October of 1912, but her "house" would be ready for her.

Robert Nott knew his wife was dying. They were inseparable, and he vowed that after death, they would remain together, not in the austere marble of a mausoleum, but in a real house. So he built one on a large lot in Oakdale. Such construction certainly would not be allowed in a present-day cemetery. Nott had the rose-colored bricks hauled to the site, and he personally mixed the mortar to build the house with his own hands. He installed the windows and hammered flooring into place.

Anna Nott died at 59, and the love story begins, or perhaps continues. She was entombed in the cozy little brick mausoleum-house. There was said to be a braided rug on the oak floor in front of the woodburning fireplace. Narrow windows near the rooftop allowed slants of sunlight. This would be no morbid tomb.

The widower had a heavy oak rocking chair brought to the little place from Huebotter Furniture Co. Every Sunday morning, he traveled the trolley to Oakdale, opened the door so Anna in her crypt could hear, and read her the funnies. They had enjoyed this pleasure during her lifetime, and he always read them to her, putting in his own dialects and wisecracks because Nott was an actor of sorts. Perhaps he had to be, because his career was a salesman, a drummer they called them in those days.

Gradually, his visits became more regular. Soon, he was taking the trolley daily to the cemetery. He would sit in his rocker on the brick porch, with the door ajar, and read the whole newspaper to his Anna. When winter chilled, Robert Nott would take his rocker inside and build a crackling fire in the little fireplace.

This continued for a remarkable, loving 10 years until Robert Nott's death in 1922 at age 72. When he died, he was entombed in the little house with Anna. In years later, when two of their children, Benjamin and Elizabeth, died, they were buried in the lawn outside their parents' house.

The house now is carefully sealed; the doors and windows covered with thick plywood. Yet, the story of Robert Nott's vigil remains more than a legend.

No descendants have been found, but with the help of Diane Cornick, and the genealogy and history department of Davenport Public Library, there is substantiation of Robert Nott's devotion.

Certainly, he was no eccentric. He came from a brilliant family. His father had been a member of the New York Supreme Court, a lawyer who had read law in the office of Martin Van Buren, who became U.S. president. Apparently, Robert was such a citizen of esteem that no less a person than Ralph Cram, publisher of the Democrat & Leader (a predecessor of the *Quad-City Times*), was a pallbearer.

Anna Nott was mourned in a melodramatic obituary that noted "her gentle spirit has passed from earth," and that she would rest in the mausoleum built for her by her husband. She, too, was a prominent citizen. Her father was a Presbyterian minister.

It is a fascinating story of love that never ended. It is as Emerson said, "The moment love becomes casual, it becomes commonplace."

ॐ

A doctor recalls the night a star fell

Some people you never forget. I think of Cary Grant every Nov. 30 — the anniversary of the night in 1986 that the Hollywood icon died in the Quad-Cities.

And I think of Dr. James Gilson, because he was the attending physician when Cary Grant died at Genesis East. Now, the doctor tells — I believe for the first time — of the actor's wishes on the night of his death.

Cary Grant, according to Gilson, was ready for his soul to rest; he preferred death to living impaired.

Destiny is a strange nemesis for all. It played a cruel trick on Dr. Jim Gilson. Cary Grant died of a massive stroke that night. In 1995, Gilson was hit by a massive stroke. At 55, he was at the peak of his career as a cardiologist.

It has been a long, struggling comeback for Dr. Jim, whose stroke was a frightening whiteout in the midst of night, leaving him with aphasia — impairment of the power to use words. For 18 months he could not talk. Now he seems to be his old self again — yet likely never will practice the skills for which he was so respected.

He has founded Alternative Health Services through Genesis West to foster hope for others who have been hit by strokes or otherwise handicapped. I sat one evening with Dr. Jim at the Col Ballroom where he and an assistant were hosting people recovering from strokes.

I visited with Dr. Jim, asking: "Remember, one 29th and 30th of November?" Certainly, he remembered.

In the afternoon of Nov. 29, Cary Grant fell ill while doing sound checks at Davenport's Adler Theatre before his appearance at the Festival of Trees Gala.

His wife, Barbara, insisted that Cary go to his room at the Blackhawk. She wanted him to be hospitalized but he refused, saying it was only a touch of the flu and that he didn't want to disappoint those coming to see his "Conversation with Cary Grant." For three hours he resisted the hospital despite the signs of a stroke. Finally, he agreed to be taken by ambulance to Genesis East.

"I saw him in the hospital, determining that he had suffered a brain hemorrhage. He was strong, but one side was paralyzed," Gilson says. "I recall so well Mr. Grant saying to me, 'I do not want to live as a cripple. I would rather die.' He repeated that. It was obvious that he was not going to fight.

"He wanted to die quietly. That, I understood, and stayed with him in the last two hours of his life. So distinctly, I remember his saying, 'I'd rather die than face life as a cripple.'"

And so, at 82, Cary Grant died in a silent sleep.

How well I recall that night. I left the Festival gala when it was announced that Cary Grant was ill and would not appear. With my wife — a good trouper — I rushed to the hospital. I was oddly out of place in a tuxedo amid news people who began trickling in from the Chicago Trib and Des Moines Register.

His official time of death was at 11:22 p.m. Nov. 29, but it was hours — actually Nov. 30 — before it would be confirmed. This left deadlines, here and around the nation, in a dither.

About 3 a.m. Nov. 30, after all had calmed down, my wife and I walked out into that cold November night with Dr. Jim. He was gnashing a pear.

Gilson put a hand on my shoulder and said, "Guys like Cary Grant are supposed to live forever." I shall never forget that eulogy.

And in the dark of that chilly morning, my wife said to me, as we walked away: "Dear, do you remember what day this is? It's our wedding anniversary."

ખ

A first — and last — ride for the Pony Man

Outside of his family, there wasn't much that Louis Marten of Long Grove loved more than his ponies. Few things gave him more pleasure than to harness up his ponies and give the kids — kids anywhere — rides in his pony wagon.

He was the willing guy who happily hauled kids at every fair or fun day.

Some kids were city-fied, and never before had known the pleasure of hanging on in a wooden wagon behind the clip-clop of ponies, waving to moms and dads while Louie firmly grasped the reins.

Louie liked when anyone called him, "The Pony Man."

And so, it would have suited Louie to a smile when he rode to his grave behind two of his ponies, Mike and Duke, in the brand new wagon that he had never quite finished himself.

Louie died, at the age of 73, while watching his four ponies in the barnyard, making sure they weren't getting too wet in a light rainfall. A half-hour earlier, he had hitched up two of them and taken his wife, Bea, for a quick ride to Park View.

"I'll keep an eye on them while you fix supper," he told Bea. She returned to the window, where he sat eyeing his ponies, and found him dead in the chair, likely from an aneurysm.

Everyone, one can suppose, has a craven fear of death. But Louie likely was more fearful of not finishing a brand new wagon he was working on for the Long Grove Strawberry Fest, held annually in June. It was polished wood, with silvery wheels, the finest he had ever hitched ponies to.

Neighbors knew of all the work he had been doing to build that new pony wagon. He'd been at it since September.

So, in the days after Louie's death, a neighbor, Ron Hilsenbeck, worked intently on that wagon. He finished the work that had stopped when Louie died.

And when Runge's hearse arrived at Long Grove Cemetery, waiting there was Louie's shining new wagon, now completed. It would have been to Lou's satisfaction. Mike and Duke were hitched up and ready to go.

Pallbearers lifted the casket from the hearse onto the wagon. Aboard, alongside the casket, rode four of Lou's youngest grandchildren.

The ponies pranced and pulled the wagon the full route around the cemetery road, then came to a halt at the burial site.

The children were smiling through tears for grandpa.

"This is the way my husband would have wanted to go," Bea says.

It was, indeed, Lou's first — and last — ride in his grand new wagon.

꿔

Mournful mooring:
A captain's farewell

So many changes, and yet it is changeless — the Mississippi. It is a morning smell, a Mark Twain-esque morning, and in the pilot house of the big President, Capt. Larry Williams is on his last run, piloting the old boat that has had about as many lives as he has lived in his 42 years on the river.

This is bon voyage run for Capt. Williams, who shipped aboard his first riverboat as a deckhand when 18 and had his licensed shoulder epaulets by 21. Williams: It is a name known up and down the Mississippi and Ohio rivers. For nearly a century most of the family have been pilots.

Capt. Williams slaps a brass rail and squeezes a monkey's fist, a strangely named ball-patterned hunk of rope that is tossed ashore to fetch a line for landing.

"Forty-two years, a long time for me to be on the river," he says. "The only time I'll be on the river now is with a little boat, fishing. They always said if a man wore out a pair of shoes working on a big boat, he'd never leave the river. I've sure worn out a lot of shoes."

And so this is the final run for Capt. Williams. A hundred mornings a year, The President must take to the river for a minimum of two hours. That is federal and maritime law.

Capt. Williams would have it no way other than to retire in the pilot house.

"She handles very well for her age, 74 years. She is still a very fine lady." Always, like a fine lady, "she."

We swing into the chocolate-brown big river, ruffled by the swift waters of Locks and Dam 15.

On this day, Capt. Williams is sentimentally quiet. He watches the boat's flag, on a pole that is a jackstaff of sorts. The flag is up and blowing, and the captain plays to the wind.

The sun is breaking out through an early morning mist. Repeating the words of Mark Twain, Capt. Williams softly says: "One cannot see enough summer mornings on the river."

How many tows, how many crossings, how many landings has this grand man of the river forgotten to count. How many storms and shadows and foggy-night worries of oaths, "Where the hell am I?"

There are few of his kind, if any, with a record so respected. He calls out, "See that lump of water above the Centennial Bridge. Low water there." He speaks of wing dams and the wonders of the river that changes but never changes.

The river is hushed, the dark trees emerging on green shores. "Feel that light draft," he says (I don't) while we pass the Rock River. Horse Island drifts by; a shypoke (nickname for a heron) wings ahead. Through the thickets of Willow Island we spot the rubble of a forgotten cabin. We idle toward the I-280 bridge, then turn around. Capt. Williams clears his throat.

"I'm going out front to the control station to bring the old girl in."

We glide to the downtown Davenport dock without so much as a wisp of a bump.

Capt. Williams wipes his glasses and props elbows on the old girl's rail, the same rail as when she was a packet (like the Delta Queen) before she was an excursion boat with Satchmo Armstrong in the band, and now a gambling casino.

Quietly, by himself, Capt. Williams leans in prayer. The Mississippi, as all rivermen know, is a holy thing.

ॐ

What does a VP carry in his pockets?

Not particularly interested in such things as relations with Russia and the problems of health care, I zeroed right in on Vice President Al Gore with relevant questions on everyone's mind.

"You know," I said, "whenever I leave the house in the morning, my wife asks if I have money in my pocket. Do you carry any money in your pocket?"

This was not your everyday type of question, and the veep was a bit puzzled, but broke into a Tennessee smile.

Vice President Gore stood up, before God and the humanity of the *Quad-City Times* editorial board. He reached into the pants of his dark blue suit and pulled out his pockets. Empty. Nothing in them. Not even a comb.

Other newsroom types were champing to ask him about important things, like crime and saving the Rock Island Arsenal, but I wanted to know more about this fellow who wants to be the next president of the U.S.A.

He is on the road all the time lately, a hectic pace, so I asked, "Do you ever call home."

"Twice today," he answered with a smiling snap. "Tipper's recovering from minor surgery and is doing fine, thank goodness. I have four kids and talk to them daily, too." They're all around the country at the moment, but he tries to track them down. Fortunately, he says, some carry cell phones.

"I called my mom, too, down in Tennessee. She's 87." He was going into detail about how Pauline came from a poor family and a Rotary Club loan helped her through college. I did not care to hear about his mom's history, and switched gears to ask if he ever drives a car anymore.

"Not often, the Secret Service is around," he answered. "But sometimes on my own, I go out."

"What kind of car do you drive," I inquired. That threw the veep for a moment until he recalled that it was a Mercury. He told of once having a Plymouth van. When he gets back to the Tennessee farm that he and Tipper own, he tools around in a GM pickup truck.

Those serious news people, figuring that their questions were going to change the axis of the universe, wanted to talk about tobacco and the FDA, but I kept rambling folksy, about going to the movies.

Vice President Gore pointed a friendly finger at me and said, "I highly recommend 'Mansfield Park.'" He and Tipper like to get rental movies (do they pay for them?) but he admitted rentals can be a gamble. Both of us agreed that we liked "Deep Blue Sea."

"You know, I liked 'Matrix,'" he said, in an almost apologetic tone.

We could have chatted all afternoon in small talk, light years distant from the problems of the world. No one else had a chance to get a word in, and at one point he said to me, which made others in the room a bit aghast: "This is the damndest interview I ever had."

Then we got down to important things, like how he has time to eat decently.

"I fly on Air Force Two. I get a lot of chicken, and you know how airplane food is. I think chicken survives better at 10,000 feet." He laughed, held his hands together in pilgrimage, and added: "Oh, I really like Iowa pork ... and corn."

Finally, I allowed the real reporters to ask questions. After a Secret Service agent came in and quietly said to the real reporters — "Only one more question" — the Vice President of the United States came over to ask me what I had for lunch.

"Tuna fish and pretzels," I said.

"No mayonnaise?" he questioned.

He signed the yellow legal pad on which I had written his choice quote: "This is the damndest interview I ever had."

He signed it "Al Gore, Jan. 3, 1999." That so, on the third day of the year 2000 he wrote 1999.

I may even vote for him, even if he's not Y2K compliant.

❧

Nile Kinnick,
who might have been ...

In the rabble-scrabble of presidential politics, have we forgotten the Iowan who could have been ... Nile Kinnick?

There is no question that this football hero from the University of Iowa and young statesman had Washington in mind.

He could have made a brilliant president, had he not been claimed by World War II. Some newspapers were once even touting, "Kinnick for president." It could have been ... not just a stadium at Iowa City in his name, but also a presidency.

Nile Kinnick was far more than one of America's greatest athletes, though in 1939 he not only won the Heisman, but in an Associated Press poll ranked ahead of Joe DiMaggio, with a batting average of .381, and Joe Louis, who knocked out all of his four opponents.

When members of Kinnick's 1939 Iron Men once held a reunion, Sports Illustrated wrote of teammate Al Coupee being asked if Kinnick — were he still alive — would be with them. Coupee replied: "No, I tell you where Nile Kinnick would be right now. He'd be in the White House. And with him there, we wouldn't have any of the junk that's going on now. Nile would've been so far ahead of these people."

When Kinnick accepted the Heisman, he spoke more like an elder statesman than a handsome young athlete who had just turned 21. In a dramatic speech, he said: "I would like, if I may, to make a comment which I think is appropriate at this time. I thank God that I was born to the gridirons of the Midwest and not to the battlefields of Europe. I can say confidently and positively that the football players of this country would much rather fight for the Heisman award than for the Croix de Guerre."

Kinnick graduated Phi Beta Kappa from the University of Iowa where he was a prolific writer and scholar, spurning NFL offers to enter law school. Even then he had an eye on a future in politics, in the footsteps of his grandfather who had been an Iowa governor. Kinnick introduced Wendell Willkie, presidential candidate, at an Iowa rally with a speech that rang with far more emotion than that of the candidate: "When members of any nation have come to regard their country as nothing more than the plot of ground upon which they reside, and their government as a mere organization ... the moral dissolution of that nation is at hand."

Sports Illustrated, in a lengthy piece on Kinnick a dozen years ago, told of the hue and cry of "We want Kinnick" at that Wilkie rally. Kinnick had a Kennedy-esque mystique, and the Marion Sentinel and a few other Iowa newspapers were already endorsing him as a future president. Kinnick became a spokesman for a young generation and wrote another ambitious Republican, Loren Hickerson: "Yes, Loren, I would like to meet you as a fellow senator or representative in Washington, D.C. Whether this ever be my lot, none can say now."

With war clouds hovering, Kinnick enlisted in the Naval Air Corps Reserve and was called to active duty a few days before Pearl Harbor. During his early days in the service, he continued as an unyielding writer, a far deeper thinker than expected of a Jack Armstrong, All-American boy type.

While in Florida flight training, he wrote in his journals on the plight of black Americans: "The inequities in human relationships are many, but the lot of the Negro is one of the worst ... kicked, condemned, ridiculed, no sense of human dignity. When this war is over ... may wisdom, justice, brotherly love guide our steps to the right solution."

On June 2, 1943, Kinnick took off from the deck of the carrier Lexington, flying a Grumman fighter on a routine training flight off the coast of Venezuela. There was engine trouble, and unable to return to the carrier, he ditched in the ocean. When rescuers arrived, there was no trace of him.

Whitney Martin of Associated Press wrote: "Why does war have to take such really human, humans. It doesn't seem fair."

A moment in time:
Quiet men at a table

They sat there so matter-of-factly at the Ox Yoke Inn in Amana, Iowa, poking at their food, so little conversation. Their wives were anxious to go shopping, but the men dawdled. There were about 30 of them at a long table in the dining room. The men were gray to bald; quite a few of them looked paunchy. It could have been a Farm Bureau gathering, but I could overhear no talk of crops.

When men in their 70s gather, there usually is the banter, "Remember when ..." or "Remember that guy who ...?" But these men were unusually silent.

One, with a heavy heave, arose from his chair. On the back of his jacket was the bright emblem of an airman who had flown in the China-Burma-India theater of World War II.

"You are a hero," I spoke to him, from a nearby table.

He looked startled.

"You flew in the toughest, most miserable territory of the war," I said.

"Don't need to remind me; we dropped 3,000 planes in those damned foggy mountains."

He said that once a year, surviving airmen of his squadron gather someplace in America for a reunion. On this day, it is in Amana.

The portly man waved an arm toward his comrades. "We don't have much to say to each other anymore."

From a folder he carefully withdrew a yellowing photo of a C-46 crew, handsome young bucks from the wild blue yonder in leather flight jackets.

"That's some of us. We can't remember when we were that young. Look at us today; a bunch of old geezers with nothing to say."

I patted him on the back, on his CBI emblem.

"We've been around Amana all day, and you're the first one to notice and know what it meant," he said with a dull look on his wrinkled face.

"Hell, does anyone care anymore?"

He ordered another beer and the wives meandered outside to go shopping.

ɔ♠

Daughter finds father's saviors

Diane Beilstein's long search is over. She has made contact with the French family who saved her father's life during World War II.

She has located Lt. Jack Beilstein's heavy leather flight jacket, too, and the St. Ambrose graduate's class ring.

It has taken Diane Beilstein, Davenport, a lifetime to find the French family who hid her father from German troops — sometimes in a woodpile — after the B-17 on which he was bombardier crashed 57 years ago during World War II.

He was badly injured and would have been shot — or, at the least, imprisoned — by the German soldiers who searched for the airman who had parachuted into a Brittany wheat field from a tumbling, blazing B-17 bomber.

This Memorial Day, at a moment when we are saluting heroes of our wars, Diane Beilstein is thrilled to have located the family who rescued her father, a highly decorated airman.

"I cried for three days after being contacted by the French family," she says. "I've written them long letters. My next hope is to go to France to personally thank them."

It is an extraordinary scenario, with many James Bond-esque surprises. It could be a TV or movie plot, of spies and suspicion and the fast heartbeats of near-capture. And it is the tale of that flight jacket and ring — Lt. Jack Beilstein's flight jacket and ring. The heavy leather jacket, with its thick wool collar, is worn today by Maurice Gautier, son of the French farmer who rescued Lt. Beilstein. Maurice wears his St. Ambrose ring, too, for good luck.

Diane has been seeking the unknown family with the help of Europeans who scan old manifests and flight records to track families of bomber crews whose planes crashed while flying to free Europe from the Nazis. Sadly, Jack Beilstein died four years ago, long before one of these search groups was able to establish the link between him and the Gautier family.

Recently, Diane trembled to open this letter from France: "I am the son of

Joseph Gautier, the French farmer who took in and hid your father following the crash of his aircraft on the 16th of September 1943. My father died in 1985 at the age of 63. I am now aged 47. My brother, myself and our families still live near the place where your father arrived by parachute on this afternoon of 1943.

"You will be interested to know that I am a teacher and an aerial photographer. I wear the flying jacket of your father during photographic missions and I still have his gold ring which figures a Greek hoplite (a heavily armed foot soldier).

"I have been, since my childhood, impressed by my father relative to the 'American pilot.' My passion for aerial photography is certainly related to your father's visit, it is true, to the farm of my parents. I have tried in great vain to contact you years ago."

Diane says: "There was a French phone number with the letter, written by someone who knew English."

Diane doesn't speak French, so a translator made contact, and the intriguing story unravels about Jack Beilstein and Joseph Gautier, the American airman and the French farmer.

During World War II, Germany occupied Gautier's native France. In 1943, Gautier was 20, trying to avoid being hauled off to Germany with other able-bodied Frenchmen to work in the munitions factories. He hid in a secret room inside a woodpile, and continued to farm near the town of Plechatel in Brittany.

When Lt. Jack Beilstein plunged into Gautier's field, the farmer was unsure whether the airman was dead or alive. He was nearly unconscious from lack of oxygen, and seriously injured his back and hip as he tumbled into the wheat field. Gautier rushed to the airman, bringing him bread and wine before helping him to his hiding place in the wood pile. There they both huddled while a German patrol searched and shouted, "Wo sind sie?" — "Where are you?"

Gautier hid Beilstein in the woodpile for days until the French Resistance forged documents declaring him to be Jacques Doleau, a French laborer.

Fearful, Resistance members wanted no trace of Beilstein's military gear.

After the airman left Plechatel, Gautier carefully buried all of his things — including his flight jacket and college ring — in a sturdy, lined wooden box. If German soldiers had found them, there was little question that Gautier would have been summarily shot.

The farmer continued to live in his hideaway until the war's end. Years later, he dug up the thick box containing Beilstein's flight jacket. It was marvelously preserved and he gave it to his son, Maurice. He also presented him the St. Ambrose ring, which is always on Maurice's finger.

Early in the air war over Europe, Lt. Beilstein was a hero making (national) headlines. With two of its four engines out on his first plane, El Diablo, he still managed to reach target and shoot down an unprecedented seven German fighters.

He won the Air Medal and six oak leaf clusters before his second plane, Hell's Bells II, was blasted from the sky. He was declared missing and presumed dead. Still, his wife, Virginia, back in Davenport, held hope, not knowing that he was in the hands of the French Underground. There, it was cat-and-mouse with the Germans.

"At St. Ambrose, he started out to be a priest, learned a little French, and went into the service," his daughter says. "That smattering of French helped him in encounters with German agents and the Gestapo."

Once, when he was billeted in a Catholic seminary, he and seven other Americans slipped away through a hidden fireplace when suspecting agents stormed the place. Before leaving France, he had the strange freedom of living in the home of a French police officer, wandering the streets, attending movies and even visiting the Cathedral of Notre Dame.

But repeatedly, he was in danger. In Toulouse, a Gestapo agent grabbed him at a railroad station and herded him inside with captured American fliers.

His St. Ambrose French bought his escape. He spoke enough to convince the Germans that he was a handicapped laborer. The others went off to prison camps.

Another time, he ended up in a train compartment with three German officers.

When they became suspicious, he muttered what he called "fractured French" and — as they dozed — slipped into another compartment.

Finally, after hiking, busing, bicycling, hiding in barns and living with civilians who risked all to hide the fugitives, Beilstein and a cluster of Allied airmen made it to the Pyrenees Mountains in the middle of winter.

They walked, and sometimes crawled, through snow up to their waists for four days to escape to Spain.

"Dad once confided in me that they left one airman behind," his daughter says. "His legs were frozen."

When they got to the safety of Spain, Diane says he told her, "I fell to the ground and cried, 'Mother Green, put on that pork roast — Johnnie's coming home.' That Mrs. Green was his mother-in-law."

Always, Jack Beilstein was reticent about his war. He talked little about his escapes and his 25 missions, and being shot down. He shared few stories with his family, and this piqued his daughter's interest in locating the family of the man who saved him. "Dad never liked to talk. I know it was because he felt badly about being the bombardier on a plane that killed many German civilians."

Jim Stopulos, Davenport, a B-17 pilot, agrees with Diane about her father's silence. "Jack was a real hero with many stories, but he never told them."

When he arrived home, Lt. Beilstein was assigned to military intelligence, advising other pilots on tricks of eluding the Germans, and how to make contact with the French Resistance. As a civilian in Davenport, he went into the lumber business.

Diane fingers a little hollow cross that she wears as a necklace. In it are bits of her father's ashes. Her brother, Peter, lives in Des Moines and treasures his dad's much-decorated uniform and wings.

As for that leather flight jacket, Diane wants it to stay forever with the Gautier family in France.

"Maybe, if I go over there sometime, I'll try it on. Maybe Maurice will let me wear it if he takes me flying."

❧

What would Steve Phillis say to you, American flag?

Two months ago he died for you — American flag — and you were draped over his casket yesterday at St. Pius Church and at Hodgson Funeral Home, Rock Island. What would Captain Steve Phillis, hero of the Gulf War, who died to save a comrade, say to you, American flag?

"It's red for love, and it's white for peace, and blue for the hope of free men."
— Garrison Keillor

What would Steve Phillis say to you, American flag? Always, the American flag, for the military in times of sunshine and shadow. The American flags on the hearse at the funeral home ... the kids from Jordan School, where you were a student, standing on the sidewalk as the funeral procession turned into the church. Ricky Coppula, a fourth grader, standing ramrod straight, holding his own American flag. What would Steve Phillis say to you, American flag?

On your stripes are written the rights of liberty and justice. The flag on Captain Phillis' casket, so perfectly straight — like a formation of A-10 warplanes. There were red, white and blue ribbons in the flowers around the casket, but the flag itself — so big, so proud — circumscribes all that is around it ... the blue field of stars, properly at the upper left hand corner of the casket. The mourners at the church sing "God Bless America," a bittersweet recessional. The flag outside at half staff. What would Steve Phillis say to you, American flag?

"The cross, the flag, are the embodiment of our ideals and teach us not only how to live, but how to die." — Gen. Douglas MacArthur

The cemetery is grim and sodden, and the relatives cluster in the despair of a moment such as this. The flag is still there, on the casket soon to be lowered into earth that is dark and cold. Air Force non-coms, smart in their white berets, step forward. They remove the flag. The gray casket is now bare. The flag is in the hands of the honor guard. Gently, they stretch the flag outright, and then fold it once, and then twice. Every motion is like precise puppetry. They fold it, turn it, fold it again and again until the big American flag is compressed into a 16-inch triangle.

They release it to Lieutenant General Thomas Baker, vice commander of the tactical air command of the U.S. Air Force. He is a major staff officer for the Air Force, offering tribute to a hero who has been posthumously awarded the nation's second-highest medal, the Silver Star. The general quietly speaks a few words, placing the flag into the hands of Captain Steve's mom.

She is a gentle, composed woman, resigned to the moment. She whispers her thanks. Her husband, a Rock Island physician, nods and his lips make the motions of a silent "thank you."

At the moment, as if precisely released from the heavens by the angels themselves, four desert-camouflaged A-10 warplanes — the same type airship that Capt. Steve Phillis flew — swoop over the gravesite. The rains abruptly stop as all eyes turn to the skies and one of the planes disappears in a sweeping arc to nowhere in the missing man formation. There is not a dry eye in sight. The tears mist in a colonel's eyes. It is one of the poignant moments of life and death in the Quad-Cities.

The American flag is now tucked into a polished, triangular wooden box.

What would Steve Phillis say to you, American flag?

"My heart is turning home again, to a land of youth and sunlight, beneath a flag where everyone is free." — *Henry Van Dyke*

And so it is over. The family and mourners have left. But while the news photographers linger on a hillside, packing up their gear, a fellow in a white Honda and wearing a blue golf coat drives up to the gravesite where workers are about to lower the casket.

He removes from his wrist a bracelet, one of those remembrances for Gulf airmen missing in action.

"Do you mind?" he asks the workers. They shrug.

Into the dark hole, with the casket, he tosses the bracelet.

One wonders what Steve Phillis would say?

❧

Walking with Paul ...

He was sitting on a couch in a corner, all alone, in a Quad-City nursing facility. He was frail, smiling and greeted us as friends though he was not aware who we were.

Paul has Alzheimer's disease, and it was our first visit to this always-courtly man who was one of my best pals.

Once, he was a king in the Quad-Cities. He was manager of theaters and found his way into ad agency work and gave birth to the Parade of Homes. Always, his kinship was the stage, and he helped found Broadway Theater League. At mid-life, Paul joined his old schoolhood chum in the reorganization of one of the Quad-Cities' major education institutions. Together, they ran the place and when the boss died, Paul was called back to help assemble the pieces of a vast empire.

And now Paul has Alzheimer's. The once brilliant mind drifts aimlessly, and he walks, walks, walks. Paul walks back and forth in the corridors of the nursing facility. Alzheimer's patients walk a lot, as if they are searching for something, a spirit gone like a wind's gust.

I write this not as a maudlin story, but a tale of tragedy when memories fade ... and the futility that it can hit any of us, any time. Live, love and be happy while you still can.

We walked and walked the halls together, Paul muttering an occasional potpourri of thoughts, but he has not lost one thing: He still whistles. It is a low, almost inaudible whistle, not of any tune, but more of a whisper through smiling lips.

Other patients would pass. Always the courteous fellow, Paul would say "hello" no matter how many times they walked by. I will always remember Paul as he used to be, the one everyone listened to when he spoke — ever so sparingly — at a meeting or a conference.

Now Paul is a faded memory. No longer does he tell stories, for his thoughts — whatever they may be — are engulfed in a shadow. I tried to jog old memories, of when we had such fun putting together the old Beaux Arts Balls or his valiant work for civil rights. There was no connection.

He admired my topcoat, smoothing the fabric. He counted eight buttons and looked up, smiling: "Eight buttons, just right."

Dapper Paul always wore bow ties, and when he left his apartment for the nursing facility, a friend gave me all of his bow ties. Many of them were new, with tags of almost forgotten stores like Richter's and Simon & Landauer.

I told Paul that I was going to give all his ties to kids at an upcoming kite contest. They could use his ties as tails for the kites, and as they were whipped by the wind, his memories might fly with them high into the skies.

He said nothing. He walked away from us into a large room where others with Alzheimer's were blankly sitting at tables. Paul stopped at each, offering a bright "hello."

Then, he softly whistled.

Addendum: Paul Ives died November 26, 1998, and even good friends were surprised at the private side of this public man. Paul never owned a car. He walked, walked, to hillside places like Lincoln Fundamental School where he tutored for years, long after retirement. He had chest-puffing pride for the military, and his request was to be interred at National Cemetery, Rock Island Arsenal. Until looking at his Army discharge papers, none knew that he had gone through World War II combat in north Africa, Italy and southern France and had been awarded a Silver Star.

෬

Down the Road

OUT in the small towns and farms, the conversation is simpler. The voices carry a wonderment and sincerity.

Small towns are a crazy quilt of people and places and unlikely names like "Ten Mile" and "Shanghai" and "Maquoketa," which has at least a thousand different spellings.

Midwest is the heart and the soul of all America, its cultures, its ways, its problems. There are few things I enjoy more than sitting at the breakfast cronies' table of a small-town cafe and listening to the men in seed caps solve all the worries of the world.

In his memorable "Middle West Country," William Carter wrote of all of us:

"While many societies seek a golden age in a partly factual, partly idealized past, only in this land would that past be found within a single life span ... so strong equated with a sense of place ... the Midwest."

Donkey ball fades, can't buck a trend

Those good old country ways can't last forever. Lots of our rural land is going sophisticate, and now — oh, unhappy day — we're facing the loss of donkey basketball.

It has all but gone to pasture in these parts.

In Morrison, Ill., donkey basketball was a big hit years ago. Sturdy, clumsy men mounted little donkeys and tried to play basketball in the high school gym. Once, the Morrison athletic boosters took on high school athletes, man and beast clomping and bonking the hardwood aboard the balky donkeys, which were wearing soft, padded boots.

Deidre Baker of Eldridge, Iowa, remembers playing donkey basketball for Tipton (Iowa) High in 1974 or 1975: "It was hard to get the donkey to cooperate, but when it did I was able to score a basket or two."

The major supplier of donkeys for this part of the universe was Bob Crosby's Donkey Ball in Chippewa Falls, Wis. It quit two or three years ago, and Crosby's phone has been disconnected.

In the hee-haw heyday of donkey basketball, the stubborn little burros were known to toss many a mayor or school principal or fire chief on their bottoms under the baskets. Donkey basketball and baseball drew big crowds of guffawing folks. It was pure rural fun.

But through the years, interest yawned. The cry of detractors had a hand, too, in pressuring a slowdown of donkey basketball. Animal rights groups say it is cruel to the donkeys, but Sandy Spicer and her husband, Jack, who run Buckeye Donkey Ball in Marengo, Ohio, consider such claims pure nonsense.

"It's ridiculous for animal rights activists to say donkey ball is cruelty. They're our babies, our bread and butter. We give them loving care, and they like to perform," Sandy says.

"Right now, the season's mostly over and yesterday we had 80 or 90 donkeys out in the pasture until school begins in the autumn. I don't know of anyone with donkey game outfits for the Midwest. We stick to Ohio and the East."

As the donkey games fade, other money-makers are taking hold. Rural towns raffle cars, promote tractor pulls and other such events. Even volunteer fire departments, which regularly sponsored donkey basketball or donkey baseball games, have turned to other venues. In a Martha Stewart manner, fire department volunteers in Welton, Iowa, raise money making gourmet omelets.

The marriage capital
of Middle America

"... married in Kahoka, Mo."

The words appear repeatedly in 60-year-plus wedding anniversary notices these days.

Why Kahoka? Reasons why ...

Return with me to the innocent years when this was a land of love, cupids and Evening in Paris perfume and every bride looked like Joan Crawford or Claudette Colbert.

Kahoka was the marriage mecca of the plains, and particularly for lovers from what then was the Tri-Cities. It was just down the road a pike, past Fort Madison and west of Keokuk and across the border to Missouri.

On any romantic day of the early 1940s, 85 or 90 couples would be joined in bliss, hurrying off to loveland (the nearest tourist cabin) with the world's first version of bumper stickers — "Just Married in Kahoka" — on their 1940 Chevys.

At the courthouse, the record for Kahoka marriages was 97 in 24 hours.

In 1942, Archie Starr, Kahoka's town clerk, turned out 6,874 marriage licenses, about six times the population of the town. He slept in his clothes on a cot of his living room because there was no telling when a couple would knock at the door for a license.

So many of these romantics were from the Tri-Cities, and my curiosity was piqued one Sunday when eight anniversary notices or obituaries noted marriages in Kahoka.

Why Kahoka? It was, in the early '40s, the nearest town to where a couple from these parts of Illinois or Iowa could rush to be married without a blood test, without waiting, and the age of consent was a childish 16.

"The boys were going off to war; there was a mad surge for marriage, and Kahoka was the closest place for a lot of people," said Gene Daniel, who was mayor of Kahoka for 20 years.

On a rainy afternoon I went calling at the Kahoka of today. The old Hotel Duer no longer offered a honeymoon suite, and there was a "For Sale" sign out front. The town has been pulling itself out of the doldrums with a block grant. Old houses — some on streets that were called "Lovers Lanes" — are looking quite classy. There are new businesses in town, which now has a population of 2,100.

But once, marriage was Kahoka's biggest business. For the kids, the clergy and the magistrates, this was a lode of love.

School boys were called runners. They'd spot out-of-town cars and guide couples to any one of a half-dozen justices of the peace who would pay the kids a dime for everyone they brought in.

Shelly Chapman, historian-at-large for Kahoka, told me during a visit: "Bakeries sold tiny little wedding cakes."

A print shop used big wooden block type to print those first-known bumper stickers, the ones that said, "Just Married in Kahoka." They were sold for 35 cents at restaurants that had oversized, two-handled "Cuddle-Up Coffee Cups" and romantic souvenir salt and pepper shakers. My old Uncle Oscar and his wife, Doris, had one of those cuddle-up cups; they were married in Kahoka when I was a punk.

After getting the license from Archie the clerk, couples easily found a justice of the peace with the help of the kid "runners." The justice's fee depended on a couple's gratitude, generally $2.

A couple with no cash once traded a wrist watch for the services of a justice named George Elmer Mohr. George went to his death with the pride that he was the only Kahoka justice to ever marry four couples at once.

One marriage is especially remembered, a young woman and a codger so creaky that he could not get out of his car. The justice wed them in the front seat.

As the 1940s faded, Missouri, too, passed a blood-test law and a waiting period. The sweet blush of a marriage mecca faded from Kahoka.

Today, on a rainy afternoon, the town is spiffing up. No longer does it look like a wilted wedding corsage.

 è&

No reason to be rushed along ...

Once, it was called the Lincoln Highway, the pavement that drove us out of the mud across America. Now, it is U.S. 30.

U.S. 30 is a highway to follow the advice of Robert Frost who said, "There is absolutely no reason to be rushed along with the rush. Everybody should be free to go very slow."

So ... now it is June, and at last we have escaped an ugly spring and we may live it up for a few months before hunkering down to frost and covering up the tomatoes.

We drive very slowly on U.S. 30, west of DeWitt. The old girl of a road is reckoned to have reached MidAmerica 85 summers ago, teaching us a new way to travel, showing that our country lay far beyond the windshield of a Model T Ford.

In the June-dusk, there has been a first cutting of hay. I have smelled no perfume as exquisite as the fragrance coming from a freshly mowed hay field.

When a twinight breeze blows, my nose is thankful for that sweet odor.

We have no destination, but perhaps a pause at Oster's, that tiny landmark at the far edge of Clarence, Iowa, a cafe that closes at the civil hour of 8 p.m.

As a June sun cashes in for the day, the old barns are stark silhouettes, reminding that however sophisticated we become, we are farmers whose ancestors plowed this land and gave it to us. Comfortable old frame farmhouses with ample front porches are far off the road, usually with a tire swing hanging from a tree.

The small towns pass by, shriveling but surviving, with Miller Lite neon gleaming from a bar or two. I reach for an old guide, the Lincoln Highway Atlas of 1924. It warns that the automobile speed limit in Calamus is 10 miles an hour, enforced, and a telephone is available. Clarence is listed as having a hotel and cool drinking water at the bank corner.

Not far from Wheatland, I stop to explore a blocked-off split in the road leading to a closed one-lane iron bridge, a rusting reminder of the original Lincoln

Highway. The crickets are especially loud in summer-song through thickets of Queen Anne's lace, soon to whiten, the same flowers that greeted bonneted women riding covered wagons across the prairie.

Lights are still on at Oster's. Once it was a service station, but now is tidy as a Dutchman's kitchen, with roses and daisies on the tables. By the front door is a sample of the special of the day so patrons can see the precise portion of what they'll be getting. There is no "What'll it be, stranger?" because no one is a stranger. Everyone knows one another, and the conversation reaches from one end to the other because there is room for only 32 customers on the padded chrome chairs.

Gary Oster, once a vocal music teacher at Wheatland High, breaks into song for the patrons, a parody of "My Favorite Things." Gary's 88-year-old mother, Arlene, is working the kitchen, not acting tired although she was up until 11:30 the night before baking cakes. In this tiny cafe, the unexpected can be expected — tonight's dessert is strawberry crepes.

"You've got to come outside before it gets dark to see what happened to the tree," Gary urges. The tree is a crab apple, where every Easter for 20 years he has fastened up to 5,000 plastic eggs.

"It was dying," Gary says sadly, "so last spring I told a dentist friend he could cut it down for firewood. I didn't say when he could do it, but it was such an inopportune day for my Easter egg tree to come down — he leveled it on Palm Sunday."

Gary waves goodbye out the front door, joined by "Aug" Knoll, the bandmaster at Cal-Wheatland Community School, who has dropped in for a snack. We drift off into the darkness. Barnyard lights are blinking on, sentinels that simply say, "Good evening." Far off, a farm dog is yipping.

In the rural night, we forget how miserably lost we are in the big cities, and wish for the slow lane of small towns within view of the vast growing fields where — on a hot eve like this — one can imagine to hear the beans and corn grow.

❧

'A songful, tuneful land' ... of names

In our Quad-City Land, idyllic — often bizarre — old town names still exist.

They are not gulped up by spreading suburbia, and in those names there is a strong sense of the past. Yellowed maps of three-quarters of a century ago, along with new maps of today, carry lyric town names — Otter Creek, Lone Tree, Shanghai, Green Island, Big Rock, Hamlet, Ten Mile.

"I have fallen in love with American town names," wrote the poet Stephen Vincent Benet.

The late Charles Kuralt, laureate of the common man, fell in love with town names, too. He wrote of them in his many books and loved to spiel their names on his "Sunday Morning" show.

Small towns have a region of the heart, a feel of the home place. How could one not smile when traveling through places — though often shriveled — with happy names like Joy, Sunbury, Pleasant Prairie, Sunny Hill, Springdale.

One can only guess how these small towns gained their names. Ten Mile must have been 10 miles from someplace, and Blue Grass once must have had grass of blue, although I have never been able to find anyone to say for certain.

Some names are obvious. Big Rock has an outcropping of rock and a spring, which is supposed to be a menace to drinkers, but bikers still drink the cool water.

Lone Tree was named for a giant old elm that lost its life to the scourge of Dutch Elm disease.

Plain View is just that; it has a plain view.

Hamlet has a name that fits; it never was much more than a hamlet.

Low Moor is said to have been named for the train rails through the fledgling prairie town — the rails were stamped to have been made in Low Moor, England.

Long Grove once had a long line of trees at the edge of town.

Coal Valley mined coal, and mines still tunnel under the outskirts of town.

For that matter, you might be tempted to stop and have your car checked in Mechanicsville.

Indian names abound, likely for the native residents who once peopled the land ... names like Camanche and Maquoketa, the latter certain to defy directory assistance phone operators who may be based in Denver. Once, the Maquoketa post office kept a log and registered nearly 2,000 cryptic spellings addressed to the Jackson County town.

Moscow has no Russian leanings, but most claim it's Indian for "moose cow."

Even long-time residents cannot explain how Lost Nation got its name. Some say travelers from Canada drifted to this region, got lost, and stayed, naming the place a Lost Nation.

In my roamings I find a certain lilt, a romance in small town names. Likely, the founders (or the first postmaster) named a town for a wife or daughter — names like Charlotte or Elvira.

One can toss a dart at a map of this region and be struck by the wealth of names on our maps — Zwingle, Scotch Grove, Toronto, Buffalo Prairie (which, long ago, actually *did* have buffalo), Fruitland, Conesville, Wataga, Media, Osco, Garden Plain, Goose Lake, Toolesboro.

Shanghai, not China, but near Alpha, Ill., is mostly just a memory, but once it was a real community named after a chicken.

Milan has no grand works by the Italian masters, and Orion defies many (including the finish-line announcer at our Bix 7) who insist to pronounce it like the constellation.

Robert Louis Stevenson called this land of ours a "songful, tuneful land."

Kuralt liked to quote Stevenson: "There is no part of the world where nomenclature is so rich, poetical, humorous and picturesque as the United States."

ॐ

Waiting and praying for Jesus in the gym

There has been no explanation for the mysterious appearance of Jesus Christ alongside a statue of the Virgin Mary in a Polaroid snapshot taken in the school gym of St. Stephen's Catholic Church. But never in memory has Streator, Ill., experienced such a stir.

Quietly, crowds are visiting the gymnasium to stand before the floodlight-lit statue of Mary, hopefully waiting for an appearance by Jesus.

Newspapers and TV stations are making visits. Mirror, the supermarket tabloid that was one of the first to break the Monica Lewinsky story, was there with a crew. WGN-TV, Chicago, has filmed the scene. TV stations from St. Louis and the Quad-Cities have been there, and media calls are coming from all over the nation.

It is a fascinating subject. Will this be another Lourdes, a place for pilgrimages? A Fatima?

The stir began when Mrs. Frank Lurz of Streator took three photos of the May Crowning, a ceremony. She used a Polaroid camera. In the final photo, Jesus appears to be at the shoulder of the Virgin Mary. Anything is possible, I reasoned, wondering about a double exposure. But that is not logical on a Polaroid.

I visited the gymnasium, a skeptic. I figured the Jesus image was a reflection of a leaded glass church window. That was impossible, I quickly found, because the gymnasium has no stained glass windows. The only reflection could be from the gym scoreboard, and that certainly carries no religious significance.

Going one step beyond, as if in a "Twilight Zone" spectrum, I took Polaroid pictures of my own of the Virgin Mary statue, from several distances, hopeful that I might catch the vision of Jesus on the picture. I didn't.

What does it all mean? Judge for yourself, but hundreds of people are making pilgrimages to see the Virgin Mary statue, and to pray. The crowds walk into the darkened gymnasium upon a green plastic floor covering. Three rows of chairs are lined across the gym to keep visitors at a distance.

There have been so many visitors that two additional kneelers have been placed behind the row of seats. People come to pray, and to slip messages into a box in front of the kneelers.

On a rainy weekday noon, I visited the statue. Seventy-six people had taken the time to register in the gym lobby by that hour; by nightfall, 300 had visited. On the Sunday before, 500 came to the statue, said Msgr. Peter Bolerasky, pastor of St. Stephen's.

"I can't explain it," he says. "All I can say is to look at the photograph and believe that Jesus was here. There is nothing tricky about it. The photograph shows. Some people don't believe the picture, and I suppose I can't change their mind, but to see is to believe. I believe that He was with us."

Streator, a city of 14,500, is about a two-hour drive from the Quad-Cities, east on Interstate 80, then south on Illinois 23. It has four Catholic churches and three Catholic schools, and many Slovak families. St. Stephen's is a large church, with 1,200 members and 170 students in its kindergarten through eighth grade school.

I asked Msgr. Bolerasky if he could recite any reason for Jesus Christ to visit Streator. Did the city have any real needs? Was there any crisis?

"We could use some better highways and more factories," he said seriously.

While we visited, quiet lines took their turn to walk into the presence of the statue.

"I would guess that some are putting notes in the box for healing or to get jobs. They are asking the help of Jesus," said the monsignor, who has served St. Stephen's for 42 years.

Around Streator, it would seem everyone is talking about the image in the Polaroid picture. I asked directions to St. Stephen's of a group of men standing outside a restaurant. They were so eager for me to visit the statue that one of them drove, and I followed, to the school gym at 805 East Lundy St.

A copy of the famous Polaroid is in a locked case in the gymnasium foyer.

St. Stephen's athletic director Milan Vargo volunteered to unlock the photo and drive me to Walgreens where an instant copy would be made. On the way, he said: "I know Jesus was there. You can pick it apart, but the picture shows Him."

At Walgreens, Jamie Tyne said, "I've made at least 200 copies of this in the last few days. One order was for more than 50."

There has been such an outpouring of visitors that church members have formed a volunteer cadre to be present and explain the phenomenon as best they can. The monsignor also is present many hours of the day. There is no carnival atmosphere. No pictures are sold. It is simply a silent pilgrimage to a statue and to a picture that cannot be explained.

The photographer who took the Polaroid has no explanation. She is not accepting phone calls, the church says, because she is weary of all the requests for interviews. She did, though, pose in front of the statue for Mirror tabloid.

While lingering in the lobby, with those who had visited the statue and had looked at the photograph, I found no skeptics.

Jim Flaherty of Mendota, Ill., looked closely at the photo and kept repeating, "Wow, wow. This is for real."

The Virgin Mary statue is surrounded by banks of flowers, arranged by a teacher, Sister Mary Magdalene. She is impressed, she says, by all the interest.

"I hope this will bring people back to God," she says.

The statue is no religious relic. It was purchased two years ago at a religious supply house. It was brought to the gym for the May Crowning and, after Memorial Day, will be returned to the second floor of the school where it normally stands.

I was asked if I had any particular feelings while in the gymnasium. I didn't, but driving home, I honestly had a strange sensation. My car was totally closed. No windows open, but for several minutes, the interior was basked with the aroma of blooming flowers.

Figure that one out, please.

❧

Touches of tears
in 10 snipped neckties

At Sneaky Pete's in LeClaire, neckties by the hundreds hang from the ceiling. For years, they've been snipped from wearers with a giant scissors by pistol-packin' waitresses in a place where neckties are taboo.

It's all in good fun (usually), but there is one new row of neckties with a sentimental touch.

For 17 years, 10 friends from LeClaire have met every Tuesday for cocktails and appetizers at someone's home, then adjourned someplace for dinner. At first it was to a taco place, so the gang became known as the TNTs, for Tuesday Night Tacos.

They tired of tacos, and began dining at Sneaky Pete's, though still claiming the TNT name. The guys never wore ties, knowing they would be snipped off as soon as they sat down.

One of the TNTs, Don Moeller, died suddenly six weeks ago. Don was a genial fellow, and would have appreciated what happened at the next TNT get-together.

"TNT members arrived for dinner at Sneaky Pete's, each wearing one of Don's neckties — men and women," says his widow, Jean.

Then, the scissors came into use, touches of tears for neckties.

"We planned on it happening, the waitress cutting off all of Don's neckties being worn by friends, and then — teary-eyed — we all sang the 'Whiffenpoof Song.'

"Now, the ties hang in a row, each with a little personal message, a memorial to Don's memory."

૨**

Still a country boy
on eve of glitzy 2000

The other day, flying out of Chicago over snow-pocked Mid-America, my seatmate asked where I was from.

"Iowa," I replied.

"Did you say Idaho?" he asked.

"Nope, Io-way."

He sniffed: "I'm from New York; then, you're from out in the country."

He expected that I would be wearing Oshkosh blue bib overalls and would spend the flight sucking on a toothpick.

His remark about me being from "out in the country" stuck but seconds, and then I felt proud to be a country boy. It has a good ring. I think that all of us are a rare breed, different from big city folks. After a century of shifts, from the Dobbin-drawn plow to the big bucks Deere 9000T tractors, from the trolley car to the Corvette. I still find myself a country boy at heart as we put the pedal to the metal and gear up for glitzy 2000.

Country boy? Yep. We have a Midwestern code of ethics that calls for caring and friendliness. I scanned my seatmate, reading Forbes magazine, and he did not care to converse any more with a country bumpkin like me.

I was born and reared in Davenport, a mid-size city too small to be anywhere near the million-class but small/friendly enough to be in the country, where cornfields grow to the edge of farmhouses. I've always lived in a land of neighborhoods, where the folks around me were almost like a family itself.

If someone got a new car, everyone gathered around to admire, and should any mother be ill, there would be plenty of potatoes au gratin and green bean casseroles fetched to the front door.

As a kid, we used to go over to "Money" Hageman's shop to watch haircuts.

When I had my own hair cut, Money (odd nickname, because I never knew him to have much wealth) would press a penny into my palm to put in the gumball machine. If I got a black gumball, he'd give me another penny. One summer, I took him for four pennies.

When I wasn't working in my dad's grocery, I slipped down to Bill Day's drugstore soda fountain for a Green River or a Cherry Coke.

The mayor was Ed Frick, who ran a tavern. There was a big neon sign in his window, "Good Beer, Served Properly," and he properly administered the needs of his city, regularly solving problems from behind the bar. My dad always insisted that he was the best mayor in history, and he would drop by for a brew and to learn all that happened at last night's city council meeting.

Yep, yep, I'm a country boy from Io-way, and proud of it. I'm so corny Midwest-Gothic that I still look up in the air when I hear a plane overhead, and at noon I eat dinner, and at night, I have supper.

People who have never lived in a middle-size or small Midwest city have missed out on a precious experience. They should try it some time. We have raced from 1900 to 2000, and I don't think we've missed a lap in the whiz-bang switch. We're still friendly, country folks.

I looked over at my effete big-city seatmate. He was snoozing, but I noticed he had switched from Forbes, and Vanity Fair now was drooped on his lap.

I could only guess that he had never heard of Midwest Living.

ॐ

After 126 years,
lights go out at Walcott Store

The wood floor creaks, a friendly creak. Floors like this are oiled, for upkeep. It keeps them looking spiffy, even if they've had a hundred coats of linseed oil. The floors of Walcott Store, general merchandise, have been creaking for 126 years, but the creak is now more of a sad sigh.

Walcott Store, which may be the longest-running retail business in the Quad-City region, is about to close.

Walcott will be without a general store. A Casey's may take up the slack.

Death of the general store has been a growing anathema, a small-town curse, losing business to big city supermarkets and malls. Brightly lit convenience corners have taken over where farm wives once bought yard goods and their husbands traded a crate of eggs for galoshes and groceries.

"The time has come for the end of the general store," says Billie Warnecke, whose family has been running the old corner place at Main and Lincoln streets for 36 years. "Only one other general store is left in Scott County, Horstmann's in Big Rock. If they go, none will be left."

At one time, every crossroads and hamlet had a general store, a gathering place where the proprietor would be not only a merchant, but psychiatrist and purveyor of all news and gossip within the county. Such a store was called "general" because you generally could get anything you wanted there.

Characteristic of all general stores, Walcott still has the grand old cluttered look and the indefinable essence of fresh produce mixed with rubber boots, spices and roasted peanuts in a paper sack, $1.69 and initialed S.I.S. (still in shell) and hardware. I slap a fly swatter from a rack, scan boxes of round-head stove bolts (flat heads, too) and finger samples from a rack of buttons. "A Button Gem for Every Need," the sign says.

Billie leans on the counter — you bring your purchases to the counter rather than wheeling them in a cart — and tries to smile.

"I'm tired. The general store business is dead. We can't keep up with the big places. We can't buy in 60-case lots. Why, the distributors even quit bringing us magazines to sell. We've taken to renting videos to keep up with the times, but nothing can really work for a general store anymore."

Billie says she thought about closing the store seven years ago when her husband, Al, died. "But I just didn't have the heart to close. The hardest thing I'll ever do will be to close this store and say goodbye to the customers."

A customer at the counter, Judy Brown of Walcott, agrees. "I don't know what I'll do when Billie closes."

It's a sure sign of closing that Billie is using up all the old receipts, the ones that graded candling of eggs. General store clerks once held eggs to a little light in a box to assure they weren't bad.

Until recent years, the Walcott store gave credit. A man's word was his bond, the Warneckes always believed, but life — even in benevolent Walcott — can be transient. Some customers skipped town and accounts went unpaid, so there has been no more credit.

Together, we stroll the old store, a dim place, as all general stores should be.

"It opened in 1875, once was a co-op, and really hasn't changed much," Billie says. She stands in one spot, and it's evident from the floor that here was the cast iron brute of a potbelly stove that once heated the whole place. "Once, we sold everything, washers and dryers and paint, and lots of clothes. We'd be open Wednesday and Saturday nights; farmers would come in, leave their list, and we'd fill it while they went to the saloon."

Clothing still hangs from racks; shelves have handkerchiefs. There are boots, but the store hasn't fitted shoes for years.

"I still have been ordering some bib overalls for farmers," Billie says.

They are the real thing, with a loop in the back for holding a hammer.

Clowning Around

SINCE childhood, I have found the circus irresistible. All that noise, all that color, all those snow cones. There are thousands of memories in a circus, and I am fascinated because it never changes one single peanut!

All the thrills are always there ... the catcher with arms outstretched grasping the man on the flying trapeze, the sweet smell of cotton candy, the pratfalls of clowns.

Always, I've had the temptation to say to heck with life and run off and join the circus, to lead a nomadic, gypsy life as a clown.

I've realized my suppressed desire. Yearly, I've taken off with the circus, sometimes a clown. "Silly Billy," they call me, and I have worked the big shows like Ringling Bros. and Barnum & Bailey and little "mud" (truck) shows like Franzen Bros.

"Right this way, ladies and gentlemen. Don't be afraid. Step right up."

It's never too late
to run away with the ...

"The circus is a jealous wench ... who kills the brightest stars in her crown and who will allow no private life to those who serve her ... destroying the happiness of their loved ones by her insatiable demands. She is all of these things, and yet, I love her as I love nothing else on earth."

— Henry Ringling North

Before it all began in Dallas, Texas, I knew it would be a tough day, a tough weekend. Dave Kiser, who has a loud voice and louder whistle as production manager, says, "This is going to be a six-pack." Everyone around Ringling Bros. and Barnum & Bailey Circus knows that a six-pack is three shows a day for two days in a row.

There is no more ethereal place in the entertainment universe than a dimly lit circus arena before showtime, its spider-web rigging and trapezes making strange, streaking patterns around the rings. Far off, I hear the roar of tigers, and in the cool of the "back yard" arena, I listen to the soft shuffle of Karen, a foxy old elephant who will soon be entertaining the kids.

Sitting on the ring curb, it is like being home again. For me, it is an emotion, a sublime thrill. Up strolls Jon Weiss, a master clown. In a few hours, he will be the first clown to be fired from a cannon, a treacherous act. He reminds how years ago, during the stand at The Mark, he tried to teach me to balance a dollar bill on my chin.

It is, indeed, an eerie morning before showtime. Performers are exercising, stretching taut limbs. Jamie Koenig, in charge of exotic animals, is in Ring One with two alpacas. The llama-like creatures have just had their weekly bath and Jamie has given their poodle cuts a blow dry, using an electric leaf blower.

I dislike alpacas, which have a tendency to spit, but she tells one of her pet performers, Kazoo, to give me a kiss. The alpaca affectionately smooches my cheek.

Coco, a milk chocolate-color alpaca, astounds. "Coco is deaf, but I've taught sign language," Jamie says. Using the language of her fingers, she tells Coco to kneel. The animal drops to its knees. Another hand sign and Coco lifts a foot to shake hands.

Circus people, I always find, are warm, considerate, family folks who rear children and themselves in the mad, many-languaged organized-melange of a circus, and often take pets with them. Into the ring before show time bound a couple of dogs, one a strange, bare creature with long, curly hair on its head. It's some Chinese breed, belongs to show boss Kiser. The dog is named Otto, for the late great clown Otto Griebling. The dogs chase each other, as if performing in circles inside the ring. The alpacas want to join the romp.

I'm arching a stiff neck and Karlene Stevens, already sparkly in her tight outfit for one of the production numbers, rubs my neck. She is masseur for the show, and the acrobats and tumblers need all the help they can get to smooth out the kinks. A circus like this is a city of 220 people, even with its own barber — one of the Ayala sisters, who twirl high in the air by their own long hair.

It's never-never land, waiting to happen. An unbelievable place.

≥●

A kiss for luck ...

Of course, she's scared
every time she fires her husband from the cannon

I'm in the arena dressing room with Laura and Jon Weiss. Jon is a star of the circus, with three children, so this dressing room is larger than most. The kids, Jonny, 6, and Nicole, 3, have their own little table and chairs and are shaping big hunks of Play-Doh into weird shapes. Max, 18 months, is happy in his stroller.

A typical family scene — except for the circus band blaring around the corner.

Mom has an ironing board set up in the dressing room and there is a sewing machine. A giant portable cabinet is tidy with the necessities of family life on the Greatest Show on Earth. When there's no performance, they live in a big motor home parked outside whatever arena dad is playing.

Jon is casual, considering that within a few minutes he will be risking his life in one of the world's most dangerous stunts — being shot from a cannon at about 70 miles an hour, like Superman in flight. And his wife is the only one he trusts to pull the trigger! She's in charge of all the mechanism, too.

Jon Weiss is a career clown by trade and the circus — never missing a bet for good old hyperbole — bills him as "The World's First Clown 'n Ball." But at the moment in the dressing room he is dad, playing with his kids while his wife is primping in her red-white-and-blue outfit for entry into Ring One with the big cannon.

"I'm only out there for seven minutes, and you'd think I'd always be ready," Laura says. She is nervous. She's always nervous before the grand finale when she fires that cannon. Laura is an ex-Ringling performer, telling how she and Jon were married in 1986 in Ring Two of the circus.

"We said that when kids came along, we'd leave the circus. But we've found that it can work. For a family, this is a wonderful place. Everyone watches out for one another, and we have a day care center and a school.

"Other wives nag their husbands about taking out the garbage; I nag him about checking the cannon," she says.

Together they walk backstage, leaving their children in the hands of a nanny. Over and over, Laura checks the working parts of the cannon; she eyeballs the rigging, always fearful of hitting it, and the position of the net where her husband is to land. It is an almighty dangerous act, the most treacherous on a show. Cannoneers have been seriously crippled.

I watch the backstage ritual. Jon buckles a tight wrap around his middle.

"The cannon shot is like a kick in the kidneys," he says. "I can sense when I have a good shot; even the humidity makes a difference. There have been a couple times when the cannon didn't work. Believe me, I get out."

Then, a poignant moment. He leans toward Laura, they kiss.

"It's for luck. Every time before a shoot, we kiss. My life is in her hands."

Jon, acting the part of a happy clown, waves to the audience before slipping into the cannon barrel. He yells a comic, "No, I'm not ready," but I see the serious look on his funnyman face. He slides into the cannon, now seeing nothing but the lights overhead. Deep inside the barrel he tightens his body, clutching arms to his chest. He holds his breath, closes eyes.

Countdown by the ringmaster. Laura says, "I'm always shaky at this point. What am I doing to my husband?"

She pushes the switch. B-o-o-o-o-om! Out he flies, after a shock like being rear-ended by a truck going 65 miles an hour.

Laura's eyes are clamped on him. Landing in the net is the dangerous part.

He flies, outstretched, like an arrow. At the last instant I watch him do a tuck, allowing his legs to flip over his head. He lands on his back, safe once again.

Laura is relieved. Hand in hand, they stroll back to their kids in the dressing room.

અ

Shoemaker with a smile

Clown Alley is a sort of sacred place in the circus, one of those off-limits meccas where only clowns are allowed. It's a territory where they make up, quick-change their goofy outfits, and hang out when not doing their shticks.

But hey, what's this? A grandmother-type, being adored and getting attention, and clowns waiting their turn to see her.

No wonder. She's the one who makes their shoes.

Makes their shoes? Of all occupations in this silly/serious world, Margarite "Marty" Scott has the silliest.

Soft-spoken Marty is America's only cobbler of clown shoes. She makes at least 300 pairs a year. They are those 14- to 16-inch long (6- to 8-inches wide) shoes that clowns wear, flippity-flopping around the arena of America's circuses.

For a clown, shoes are an image as significant as a bulbous nose. When a clown tears around doing 1,000 shows a year, he can wear out a pair of weighty shoes in a hurry. That's why every clown in America turns to Marty when he or she needs a new pair of shoes.

I caught up with Marty in Colorado Springs, Colo., while spending a few days with the Greatest Show on Earth.

"Hey, Marty is on the show," calls Ben Johnson, a white-face clown. Those buffoons are falling all over each other to see Marty, who makes an occasional (often long) trip to a circus wherever it might be playing to cater to the clowns' shoe needs. Marty and her husband, Wayne, a former Ringling clown, have their clown shoe "factory" in an unlikely sounding wide spot in the road called Howey in the Hills, Fla.

Marty and Wayne have the shoe sizes (regular feet fit inside those enormous waddling clown shoes) of likely 98 percent of the clowns in America. Clowns everywhere send them outlines of their feet, which Marty carefully files.

Before the Ringling Clown College closed in 1998, Marty would spend days measuring and fitting clown shoes for the graduating class. Clown College alone supplied the Scotts with measurements of more than 2,500 clown feet.

Then there are the clowns on the big tented Clyde Beatty-Cole Bros. Circus and the Big Apple Show in New York's Central Park and hundreds and hundreds of clowns who work independently.

It's a jokey time talking to Marty in the midst of a bunch of clowns. Bryan Fulton, a clown with orange straight-up hair, is getting his feet measured and traced on a sheet of paper. "Oh-oh-h, that tickles," he squeals, an exaggerated clown howl. He needs new soles on one of his pairs of clown shoes; a hurry-up job. Marty will ship them to the circus soonest from her Florida shop.

"It takes seven different machines to make a pair of shoes," Marty says.

"Maybe I will spend three or four days to cut and stitch a pair. Really, it's all hand work."

The clowns willingly pay her $200 to $250 for a custom pair of shoes; she insists on only leather.

Her trade is self-taught, and beyond clown shoes, she turns a few dollars doing high-top shoes for opera companies. "Like clown shoes, it's a craft without competition."

Her smile is one that cannot be wiped like greasepaint from her face. "I love what I'm doing, making clown shoes, because I know those shoes are going to make people laugh and be happy. Can you think of a job that is more satisfying?"

᠀

Big hips?
Everything about Zusha is big

Hip-hip-hooray!

Allow me to introduce you to Zusha, Queen of the Nile ... good circus spiel for a hippopotamus. The only hippos I've ever known were named Lotus, because they are supposed to have once lived among water lilies. Also, they were bally-hooed as "blood-sweating" hippos. They perspire, and their sweat has a rusty hue, and so the inventive P.T. Barnum coined the phrase, "blood-sweating hippos."

Every circus hippo I have ever known was mean.

And then there is Zusha, who just may be the only performing hippo in the world. No one can truthfully say this, because circus people are known to be masters of hyperbole.

Zusha, who drools a quart whenever she opens her mouth, is undeniably cute in her own way. Here's a hippo with personality. Never — except Zusha — do you see one chasing a clown or prancing around the center ring with baboons flip-flopping on its back

Zusha, who actually responds to her name like your pet dog, is the most pampered critter since the storied circus days of Gargantua the Great, the fierce Ringling gorilla who traveled from city to city in his own custom-made, glass-enclosed air-conditioned wagon.

Animal rights people might like to know that Zusha never had it so good. She has her own giant double-length wagon-trailer with a deep swimming pool.

From overhead — in or out of the water — she is misted with water, like a sprinkler system. In a big adjoining cabin-like section of her rolling home, her friends, the baboons, live in simian style. Baboons — infinitely smarter than monkeys — perform with Zusha, jumping off and on her back, waving flags or riding little hobby horses on the ring curb.

Zusha's owner is Tofik Akhundov, from Ukraine, and he speaks not a word of English. An interpreter helps keep the dialogue running. Tofik, whose teeth shine with great amounts of gold, is gleeful to talk about his partner.

"Every hippo I've ever met has been mean," I tell Tofik.

"My baby is not mean, but it all depends. Mostly, she is very sociable," he says.

Outside her cozy mobile home, the trash shows that she has just finished supper — commercial-size kidney bean cans and peas and empty cartons of Apple Flips. It is twinight, and Zusha has knocked off about a hundred pounds of vegetation and sweets, along with a big pot of wheat porridge.

When I ask to take a peek inside her quarters, Tofik and a helper swing open some heavy doors.

Zusha sticks her head from the mobile swimming pool. She snorts, hisses, grunts, growls, honks and let go with a big ba-ho-ho-ho. It has been measured at 115 decibles, which is equivalent to standing five yards away from a heavy metal band.

"See," says Tofik, "listen to her roar; she likes you."

While I call, "Nice girl, nice hippo," one ear turns forward and the other twists backward. Hippos are like that. My, what big teeth you have, and wotta mouth!

Tofik knows all there is to know about hippos, because he has had Zusha since a baby, about the size of a big pig.

"Only the whale has a bigger mouth," he says. "See, the teeth?" I sure do. I question if he has actually taken count, but he insists she has 38 to 40 teeth. The big ones (tusk-like lower canines) grow to 20 inches and weigh about five pounds.

Her girth, by way of mention, is about 10 feet.

"Where and why did you get a baby hippo?" I ask Tofik.

"I was an acrobat with a Russian circus, but acrobats can't last forever, so I wanted a new act and bought and trained this baby hippo. She is very smart. Sometimes, she is too clever. I found her at Quebec Zoo in Canada.

"What a sweet baby she was. Only a year old. She was born in 1982, and look at her now. She weighs almost two tons. I know that. We had her weighed not long ago. Zusha is lucky to be with us. In the wilds, hippos may live only 15 or 20 years. With me and the circus, she is good for 50, at least."

The tall and short
of life under the Big Top

Gee, as someone who has been called "Shorty," it's really something to look down on someone who is really short.

Michu, the smallest man on earth, looks up to me and asks, "How's the weather up there?"

That's his standard gag for everyone taller than he is. But then, everyone is taller than Michu. At 33 inches, he reaches my belt line.

I'm backyard, backstage, back everywhere at Ringling Bros. and Barnum & Bailey Circus with this fellow who is paired as a ploy with Khan — at 8 feet, the world's tallest man.

Michu is a charming little person. Some have found him diffident; I think just the opposite. After a couple days of bantering back and forth, we are good friends.

Khan, a silent, gentle giant, is the opposite. He is enormous, with a size 20 shoe, and not exactly gregarious. Let's call it shy, but I learned some things about him.

Where did the Greatest Show on Earth find this pair of so many extremes?

Michu has been a showman for as long as his tiny life remembers. He is home again with the Ringling show after Hollywood and TV stints.

As to Khan, that is a bizarre tale. No one says officially, but it's whispered to me that Ringling talent scouts found him driving a cab in Miami, Fla.

We're ready for the circus grand entry. Khan and Michu (Mee-shu) are side by side, making ready for the spectacle. Michu mocks, tightens a fist that is about as big as a golf ball, and raises it toward the giant.

Michu winks at me and, in his little voice, says: "I could whip the heck out of him if I wanted to."

Michu is no dwarf; he is an absolutely normal mortal, except that he is so tiny. He is 7 inches smaller than P.T. Barnum's legendary Tom Thumb, but wants to be a part of our tall world. I look upon him that way. Maybe that is why we get along so well. He asks for no special treatment, refuses to have anything scaled down to his size.

"Why do you look so tired?" he looks up to me. "Not me, I'm never tired," he says, outstretching the arms of his spangled outfit. "We have a third show to do today, and look at me dance. Really, I'm very continental."

He does a few waltz steps, then kicks his child's size-5 blue leather boots to perform a Cossack dance. He pauses. "Who is this?"

I introduce him to my wife. He reaches up to grasp her hand. He kisses it once, twice.

"You see, I'm very continental," he repeats, and is quite taken by my wife, who finds him charming.

Backstage, engulfed by the blare of the circus band and the spangle-bangle of circus life, Michu is a speck-size celebrity. It is a humanity of ponderous pachyderms and clowns whacking at each other and high-stepping horses. I fear that Michu will get trampled, but he adeptly side-steps. With him much of the time is Roland Szabo, who "parts the waters" for him in the melee of the circus.

It is nearing time for another of Michu's appearances in the big, bombastic arena, so large that it only accents his miniscule size.

From a sack he pulls carrots, swiped from the elephant tent. With precision, he chop-chop-chops the carrots into tiny slices and stuffs them into his red velveteen jacket pockets. A silvery carriage emerges, to be pulled by a pony named Buddy. The pony nuzzles Michu, following him in a twice perfect circle as if a ballet routine. Michu feeds the carrots to the taffy-colored pony.

He hops like a 10-year-old into the carriage, licks fingers to smooth his straight hair, and heads into the arena while the band strikes up a triumphal entry.

"Michu is one of the great assets of the circus," says David Kiser, public relations coordinator and do-everything guy for this pack of 300 circus people. "He never misses a performance and does several turns each show. He's quite a fashion-plate."

After a performance in one city, I was chatting with Michu. He was in a Chicago Bulls cap and a sports car jacket. It was so noisy around us that he suggested he climb on my lap so we could talk better. I tell you, we're pals!

What of the private life of the smallest man on earth?

His age? A secret, but I'd guess him to be in his 40s. Married? Never.

"I don't stay on the train. Wherever we perform, I stay in a hotel or motel with Roland," he explains. "No special bed or chairs or anything for me. I just fit in. Sure, I'm small and don't eat like you do. If I order a bratwurst, I eat just this much." He holds his little fingers about an inch apart.

"TV? Oh, I like cartoons."

A clown teases, "G'wan, I think you're a fan of 'Baywatch.'" Michu blushes, covering his face. He would reach less than thigh-high to some of the long-legged beauties on the show.

Michu is Hungarian, from a family of little people, all circus performers.

His parents were only 6 inches taller than their son. In 1973, Irvin Feld and son, Kenneth, discovered Michu and amid much heraldry and hoopla, brought him to the United States as a headliner rivaling Tom Thumb, the Great Wallendas, Jumbo and Gargantua. Michu stayed on the show several years before turning to Hollywood, playing in the costume worn by the title creature in TV's "Alf."

Now, Michu is back with the circus. "I love to perform. I love the applause. Ringling Bros. and Barnum & Bailey is where I belong."

Back to that giant, Khan, quite an opposite to gregarious Michu. He is from Pakistan, and is not pleased to talk much on this day because he has a sore throat. That would be a big throat to be sore because he weighs 380 pounds.

He hedges about once being a cab driver, insisting that he was more of a supervisor. Still, the story goes that he did drive, with his seat stretched back from there to eternity. Reluctantly, he slaps me five, and my paw is dwarfed in his, I ask: "The season is winding down. What are you going to do when it's all out and over?"

He says he is going to become a professional wrestler.

The final spec has ended and Michu is getting a ride to a hotel and Khan is going to his 42-foot RV where he lives with his ordinary-size wife. He says it was an arranged marriage. Their mobile home is some rig. It has 9-foot ceilings, with a specially made bed nearly 9 feet long. His showerhead is attached at 8 feet.

"I'm comfortable," he says. "The bathroom sink is so high that I don't have to shave sitting down."

ॐ

Seasonal Musings

OUR seasons have so many faces — a lone maple in scarlet on a MidAmerica hillside, the chill bones of winter with its bare oaks that look like an etching.

In summer, the stillness is broken only by the song of meadowlarks and we are caught in an endless romance ... the season to release our feet from shoes, to run through the sprinkler. People always sound much nicer in summer.

Spring is something else, a rush and a time of sensory delights ... careful now, don't scare the baby robins in the nest. Spring, when daffodils dance their yellow ballet and church bells chime as ice-locked streams gurgle in an awaited melt.

I feel sorry for people who live in Arizona or California or Florida and cannot experience the thrill of the seasons.

I take my winter gladly, but await spring as a fresh experience.

Not quite a holly-jolly day

Fa-la-la-la-la, deck the halls, 'tis the season to be jolly and light up the outdoors. Everyone's obligation is to have lit-up icicles hanging from the eaves and twinkles where once were leaves.

Everyone must be acrobats or Thomas Edisons, or they have gone mad.

I have gone mad.

"Look at all the others. Look at Mary's house," my wife hints. "Our basement is full of boxes of those little lights we had on the trees before moving into the condo."

They were in bundles, wadded bird's nests of wires, a dozen wads. Outstretched, they would stretch all the way to Eldridge.

I plug in each bundle; voila — a sparse twinkling of lights. Ha!

But then I try to unwind, to disentangle, to string them out as smooth as a comb. The more I try, the worse it gets. I sit on front stoop, ready to cry.

"You have *no* patience," my wife calls out the front door. I knew that. What is wrong is not me, but the tangles that Satan himself did to those strands.

There is a burning of my spirit.

Oh, shucks ... I shall just twine them, every single connected strand, snarled or not, working or not, around limbs of the little crab tree by our drive. It looks acceptable. I am pleased. The strands that don't light, I wind up into a fat roll about the size of a soccer ball and tuck into the low bare limbs by the trunk. Some day, I say, I shall put a red bow on it and admirers will think it is some avant garde holiday gift.

Wife, in disbelief at what I have done, helps me untangle and throw out the dead, unlit strands and do the tree over again.

"You men are all alike. You can't do anything by yourself."

There is one strand left. I stretch it around the little Norwegian blue spruce by our front door. How nice it looks. The lights worked when I tried them.

Now, only half of them light. Oh, hell. Leave 'em. By now, I am muttering foul oaths every 30 seconds.

My wife reappears — all smiles — with boxes and boxes of Add-A-Set Mesh Lights. A Martha Stewart-type is pictured on the box, stretching them upon evergreens as easily as you put a scarf around your neck. Others may find it child's play. To me, it is a bad dream maze, tangling and stretching as if I am a Mississippi River fisherman unraveling nets to catch carp.

I back up, stepping on, crackling some lights. That is seldom a prudent thing to do. Neighbors walk by, complimenting my effort and thanking me for the spirit-of-the-day Christmas music on my boom box. "Joy to the World" is intended to balm my frustrations. I smile back before returning to those accursed, treacherous mesh lights.

When all else fails I read the little directions which the Chinese — who made the lights — had assiduously tucked into the box. Believe me, there are 40 numbered bits of instructions. No wonder I am berserk.

Darkness is falling over all. Three-fourths of a chill day has elapsed, but now I have them all plugged in, ready to glow. Huzzah. Come sing a hail-heigh ho. The lights gleam — even one unexpected orphan strand that blinks on and off every 20 seconds.

Gusts of surprise, and kisses from my wife!

ॐ

Is there anything good about winter?

These are the days when we begin counting toward spring, particularly because it's been a hard-knock winter. How many times did you slip-slide fall down? How many times were you hip-deep in the snow as the plow operator clogged your driveway? But look at it this way. It could be worse. There are some good things among the awfuls, so long as you don't look at your utility bill.

The good of winter ...

Bad weather keeps the riffraff out of town; they stay where it's warm.

There are no ticks, mosquitoes or yellow jackets while you hike at Black Hawk State Historic Site. No nettles or poison ivy.

Water is colder coming out of the faucet.

There is the comfort, on a chilly night, of crawling into bed, preferably with a warm body beside you.

There is a snug feeling about February, the peace of coming inside to a warm fire in the hearth. There is this thing about a hearth: It calls for small company, for companionship. No essence can quite compare with this, the redolent smell of woodsmoke at night.

February is a time for looking out the window and seeing that in a couple of months it will be time to cut the grass again.

In winter, taking a walk in the woods feels more of an accomplishment when the wind is biting at your face and the snow is crunching under your feet like potato chips.

Winter is the challenge; June is for wimps. John Steinbeck said, "I've lived in good climate and it bores the hell out of me. I like weather rather than climate."

Think of it, you can drive all the way home from Whitey's or Culver's without your ice cream cone melting.

The best air show in winter is free — the eagles, soaring silently like kites over our riverfronts.

And one last poetic irony, winter's snow has its advantages: It hides all the scars of the Quad-Cities.

ॐ

The hope of June

When the days stretch on for-glorious-ever

Here we are! This is it! Let's not hang around and wait until 9:03 a.m. June 21, the first day of summer. This is the real June 1. This *is* summer and that rhymes with funner. Let's all get into the middle of it.

Kick off your shoes. What's better than walking in grass in your bare feet?

Who knows, the sun may even be shining and by the end of the week you'll look two shades tanner.

Why, now that summer is here, you'll even sound like a much nicer person on the telephone.

Hurry, spread out a lawn chair before all the shady spots are taken. Or, go to a park and listen to the glorious kid-chant of the Little Leaguers, "Hey-batter, hey-batter, hey-batter."

We've had enough rain, but turn on the sprinkler and run through it anyway. You can always make it look like an accident.

The dandelions have run their course, and about all that's left of them are puff-balls. Be a kid again. Blow on them and make them feel needed. If you chance upon one that is still blooming, pick it. Hold it closely under the chin of a child and say, "Butter."

There still is time to plant zinnias, but it's too late for morning glories.

And put out little lids of beer under your hostas to attract the grubs. They say they love beer and drown in the brew. (They say.)

Ignore, for a whole day, the messages on your answering machine. Drive to the top of Prospect Park in Davenport, a romantic knoll, and watch the sailboats skimming like waterbugs on the river. At mid-afternoon on a weekday, you may be lucky to catch the concert of a guitarist. The guy shows up daily, between 2 and 4.

Get out the grill. There's nothing like a juicy steak or burger grilled outside. Be exotic. Sprinkle some herbs on your burger. There's nothing like a burger with a tall, cool glass of lemonade.

Which reminds of a vintage Marx Brothers joke to close all of this out:

Groucho (on the bench as a judge): "Eliminate that testimony."

Chico (the witness): "Great. I'll have a glass of eliminate, too."

&

The importance
of clearing a garden ...

There is no homily in this, but to begin clearing a garden — as I did last week-end — is like a good preacher's message from the pulpit. It is fodder for the mind, and a proposal of thanks and future hope.

Life is like that.

We have been blessed with a nonchalant autumn, clear as the crystal on grand-pa's watch, and then came rain to green some lawns that were beginning to look like toast.

The pink impatiens in the flower boxes of our deck are beginning to act like they've done their duty for the summer. Can frost be far behind? I have been pulling the long stiff stems from the rows of day lilies beside our house. They are like tan reeds, and I have been told to pull them, or they will not bloom next summer. I question this, because I have yet to see a farmer pulling dried stems from the orange day lilies that bloomed in the ditches.

I have been trimming to ground-level the hostas, and stuffing their leaves into big brown bags for the city to pick up. The hostas have been drooping, but these amiable plants — gifted to us by neighbors — have summered well and should be bright and cream-edged come springtime. It is good to have neighbors. Another neighbor volunteered to help me cut down a spruce that has sudden-ly lost its blue needles and obviously is all but dead.

This is our first full autumn in a condo out Forest Grove Road way in Davenport, and I confess at times to missing our big two-acre yard in Bettendorf. But I will not miss the back-break of raking leaves. Our condo has a just-right size yard, and the yellowing leaves already falling from our copse of birch trees will be no major problem.

While I made a few false starts at raking, I thought of next year's future and the joy the flowers had given us in a summer that seemed just right. No blistering scorches without end, no root-wrecking downpours. Next season, we will be planting into the millennium. Who would ever have thought that we might live to see the year 2000?

The fallacy that we may in some way control Mother Nature sinks into me every autumn when I clear garden. Without much real help, the glance of a flower, as naturalist John Muir said, "controls the greatest of creation's braggart lords."

As I drive to work in the morning, I see an abundance of goldenrod along Forest Grove Road, which doesn't have any forest that I can see. The ditches, Mother Nature's own personal garden, reminds of Bliss Carman's poem, "An Autumn Garden" ... "Of aster and goldenrod, tilled by the rain and the sunshine, and sown by the hand of God."

Firebushes are showing off, and though our condo-yard is already amply planted, I found a sale at a local nursery. They had sturdy plants, at an agreeable price — firebushes as crimson as a Red Delicious apple — and I will find a place for one of them. I must find space, too, for my favorite tree, a lacy-leaf Japanese maple.

The earth is so soft after this week's rains, and soon I must plant sacks of daffodil bulbs. They are the flower of life. Last fall, I planted a batch of daffodils, sprinkling the bottom of the holes with some powdered invigorator, being careful to follow instructions that each bulb should have fertilizer the size of a dime. That is difficult, sprinkling out of a box with a hole the size of a quarter.

While tending to my autumn chores, I'm reminded that a season's future rises and falls, forward and backward, almost with the tick and tock of the daylight-saving time clock that will strike next month for the last time of the 1900s.

Clearing my garden for winter is a good feeling. Perhaps my little garden is the rhythmic feeling of life itself. Perhaps it is like a good preacher's sermon ...

ॐ

Our Towns

MOST of us never think of it this way, but we are really fly-over people. That's how Bob Greene, the Chicago newspaper columnist and author, describes us in his introduction to "Calling the Midwest Home," a lively look at origins, attitudes, quirks and curiosities of America's heartland.

Greene sets the pace for Carolyn Lieberg's book (229 pages, Wildcat Canyon Press) when he describes fly-over people ...

"It means what it sounds like. We are the people whom the so-called power elite on both coasts fly over on their way back and forth to meet with one another ... They don't even mean 'fly-over people' to be a particularly demeaning description, although of course it is ... What they don't understand — what they will probably never understand — is that some of us like being people who are flown over. Because if you are a fly-over person, you by definition have your feet on the ground. It's one of the inherent qualities that comes with choosing to live in the heart of the country."

A naked woman and an ice jam

It could be the strangest call a mayor ever got. The sheriff said to the mayor of Buffalo, Iowa:

"You better get down here, your honor. There's a naked woman on the ice."

In all the misery of our frequent floods, this one moment emerges as blushing mirth, a real spoof during agony. It was such diversion from sandbagging that it claimed national TV and headlines around the nation — but no photos, if you please, in print or on the telly.

The whole scenario is something that could have been dreamed up for a "Saturday Night Live" sketch.

In the year 1966, a stubborn ice jam clogged the Mississippi River. It began below Locks and Dam 15, with boxcar-size floes of ice so mighty that heavy iron railings were ripped from LeClaire Park. The ice heaved downstream in massive chunks, spilling water ashore. Down toward Buffalo, a flood level of 18 feet was reaching town and country.

Into the mess stepped the naked woman.

As a promotion stunt, an entrepreneur for the Seahorse Lounge on 11th Street, Rock Island, engaged one of his mermaids — who usually performed in a big aquarium behind the bar — to stand on the ice in Buffalo. She was a bosomy maiden, exposed from the waist up, supposedly such a hot number that the ice would melt. The promoter had called every newspaper, every TV station within miles.

It was a timely charade, inasmuch as other suggestions for unlocking the ice jam were not working. Dynamite was out of the question. One idea was to have National Guard planes fly low over the ice, spreading charcoal to hasten the melt.

But back to the naked woman on the ice.

The Scott County Sheriff's Department had been alerted, and Sheriff William "Blackie" Strout was present to eye the situation.

Miss Ice Pick posed smiling and shivering. Newsies ogled, photogs were wary, all realizing that their editors would never allow such nudity in print or on the air.

Jack Stalder, then mayor of Buffalo, recalled it all years later.

"I was working in construction on a job at Ralston Purina when Sheriff Strout called. He said, 'Mayor, I've got a naked woman in your town of Buffalo, standing on the ice with a pick. What're you going to do about it?'

"This was February, and I had been mayor for only a month," Stalder remembered. "Green as could be, and here I was faced with this nude problem. I came right down and all I could do was arrest her. Being a small town, I acted as judge and took her into mayor's court. What a time! All those curious reporters."

Miss Ice Pick, who claimed other names like Miss Aqua Maid, was given an overcoat and a hearing before Mayor Stalder.

"She was shivering, a pleasant person who was just going along with a naughty promotion scheme. We took her to City Hall, and I felt that a fine was in order. I looked at the statutes; the charge would be indecent exposure. I fined her $100, or 30 days in jail. Someone must have paid, because she was released.

"I know when the National Guard pilots — who were spreading the charcoal in the middle of the river — saw what was going on, they flew in low."

The river crested a few days later, Feb. 21, 1966, at 18.3 feet.

Other crests will come and go, but none like the crest with the naked woman.

Jack Stalder laughed: "I remember that she had a nice body."

❧

Afloat, alone aboard
a forgotten President

"Who-o-o-o-o-e-e-e." I cup a hand and holler across the old steamboat's engine room, while standing spookily beside pistons that are big as a new Chevy and as old as I am. I wait for an echo back from across the boiler deck where one of the oak pitman arms is intact. Those arms, moving back and forth, pushed the paddlewheels to their tap-a-tap-a rhythm. All is silent.

I am the last man aboard the ghost steamboat, The President.

While cohorts of the media were scurrying for a first look at the new Rhythm City casino on Davenport's levee, I chose to visit her predecessor, the old girl, The President, tethered so forlornly alongside.

No one is paying a lick of attention to her.

She is a ghost ship with an indefinite future.

She saw more millions of dollars change hands than anyone will talk about, much the less count. A decade ago, she was the toast of the town. Once, she was a peacock; now, she isn't even a feather duster.

Down temporary wooden stairs I climb, from the gaudy glitz of Rhythm City into the forlorn President's water-level boiler deck. Always, this grand old side-wheeler stubbornly held to its Mark Twain-esque roots. Its reminders as the queen of excursion boats are still anchored in the ship's bowels. Levers tell "ahead" and "astern." Over there is the little windowless cabin where Israel Gorman lived for 58 years of his life, oiler (engineer) and guardian of the boat he claimed as his own. Were Issy alive today, he would still be there, right at my side.

Up carpeted stairs I climb, clinging to brass railings that still shine, into the soundless main casino. I imagine ghosts of gamblers past and the flaring cornet of Satchmo Armstrong, who once played in this room with Fate Marable's jazz band.

I expect grim darkness, but no! Except for an octopus maze of disconnected wires on still-soft carpeting, and some slot stands, the levels and balconies of this old casino are electrically alive. The old girl is reluctant to call it quits without a showy splash. I wonder why no one has thought of turning out the lights. The crystal chandeliers are bright with light, a slight sway from the waves; strands of little Italian lights arch alongside the golden gee-gaws. Neon dazzles "Jumbo Jackpot Today" and empty cages glare "Cashier."

But all is so mute, so calm, so silent. It is shivery as I stand there — so alone — as if in a Stephen King novel about a ghost excursion boat born again as a casino and now a transcendental aging grandmother-like mirage on the Mississippi.

There clings the reek of cigarette smoke; it is worn into the carpeting and the cloth wallcoverings, into the bones of the old boat itself. High on a wall, painted in a big bowed niche, is a mural of the steamboat Cincinnati.

The President once was the Cincinnati, a trim excursion boat that worked the Ohio River.

It fell on hard times and was bought and rebuilt, by Rock Island's Streckfus family of steamboat legend, into The President. That was the year 1924, when the band aboard was jazzing up a new hit, "Tea for Two."

The wheel house, from where poetic pilots could never see enough dawns or dusks, is emptied of its masters. The levers that steered the boat are straight-forward; the radar screen is dark. No one peers from the pilot's tall chair and the liar's bench, a traditional couch for visiting pilots, is without guests.

From the upper deck, on this cold windy afternoon, I stare down on the boat's giant bell. It came, without question, from the old Cincinnati, and before that likely graced the bow of some other boat that went to steamboat heaven. It had a crisp, clear tone because when cast, it likely had 100 silver dollars tossed into the molten. Silver clarified a bell's sound, old steamboat men were convinced.

I wander, feeling so alone, keeping company with this old girl that everyone has suddenly forgotten. She and I are exactly the same age. I thought she might say, "So long," as I heaved myself back onto the glitzy successor at her side.

The turkey that came to dinner ... and stayed

Jaws drop when strangers see this big, fat turkey hurrying to meet kids at the school bus out Trout Valley way in Bettendorf. The kids pat Gobbles, and he follows a few of them around the neighborhood.

"You should have seen him last winter when we took him sleigh riding," says Morgan Lintz, 8, daughter of Mike and Lisa Lintz.

Gobbles is a perfect pet, one that never runs away and is no bother. He even has gone for a ride in the van with the family, who live on Bettendorf's Forest Grove Road, an acreage in rural green suburbia.

"He'll never be housebroken, so Gobbles stays outside. Other than that, he's as tame and friendly as our two dogs and cat — and all of them get along just fine," says Lisa Lintz. "It's a strange relationship. You'd think they'd go after each other, but they don't. Odd, too, Gobbles never runs away, even though our place is unfenced."

This extraordinary turkey was spared from the roasting pan by the Lintz children, Morgan and Michael, 5, who — like all kids — love birds and animals.

Gobbles arrived for Thanksgiving 1999, given as a gag gift to friends of the Lintz family.

"The turkey was straight from the farm, and the landlord wasn't going to allow such a thing our friends' apartment, so they gave it to us," Lisa says. "They intended for it to be our Thanksgiving dinner, but we found the bird to be quite tame. Besides, we had just moved here from California, and it was cool for us to have a live turkey."

Gobbles quickly was domesticated. He wanders the neighborhood and has become a bird of habit. He knows to strut over to a neighbor's roadside mailbox at twilight for hors d'oeuvres. Regularly, they leave cheese balls for him to nibble.

And when Morgan had an outdoor birthday party, there was Gobbles, right in the midst of the kids, pecking at the wrappings and ribbons and generally enjoying himself, as only tame turkeys can do. The kids patted him. He gobble-gobbled back.

"Turkeys don't like shiny things; they peck at them, especially nail polish. So we painted Gobbles' nails and it just about drove him crazy," Morgan wrote in a report assigned by her second-grade teacher, Jane Reitz, at Hoover Elementary, Bettendorf.

Morgan explained in her essay how the turkey was saved ... "My brother and I liked the turkey so much that we didn't want to eat it. We kept feeding it, and it didn't feed us. We bought a turkey from the store for Thanksgiving."

Last winter, Gobbles was outside in the deep snow with the kids, so dad put him on the sled with Morgan and a friend. "We went halfway down the hill together," she says.

There's the old Thanksgiving ditty, " ... Over the river and through the woods, to grandmother's house we go." Last Thanksgiving, Gobbles sat contentedly in the van while the Lintz family drove to grandma's house (Nancy and Gene Meeker, Davenport) for Thanksgiving dinner. Gobbles hung around the Meeker yard for awhile, then crossed the street where he gathered quite a gaggle of fascinated onlookers.

"Gobbles is really a smart bird," Lisa Lintz says. "What's unreal is how on some days, he knows to meet the kids at the school bus. Just like a dog. The kids aren't afraid to touch and pet him. He's brought a lot of laughter and conversation to our friends and family. We hope there will be many more years to come.

"We don't know how long turkeys live, but be certain, this one is never going into the roasting pan."

Carp on a car? It's no fish story

On roads along the Mississippi River, just about anything can happen. Mark Twain was the master spinner of river tales. He would have liked this one and wouldn't have had to stretch the truth.

Early on a Sunday, just as dawn was breaking, Samantha Schillinger and her husband, Shawn, of Bettendorf, were delivering the *Quad-City Times*.

"We were in Pleasant Valley, driving along 246th Avenue when there was a big thud. A real clunk," says Samantha.

"It was scary, and I told my husband, 'Really, I didn't hit anything!'

"It puzzled us, because we couldn't see anything. It was a thud, and felt like something hit the roof, hard."

The Schillingers pulled over to check their Dodge Neon. No dents, but blood on the roof. They looked at the road where the "thud" happened.

There it was, a 3- or 4-pound carp that had come out of the sky and hit the car.

"There were all kinds of eagles on the river when we were delivering papers. We saw one in a tree over the road. What happened, we're sure, is that an eagle had a big fish in its talons," Shawn says. "Maybe it couldn't hold it. It must have been right above us and dropped that fish right on top of our car. Weird. Fish falling from the sky."

No more need be said. The first confirmed, honest-to-goodness true fish story.

૨**

Hold it ... flash! One more picture

A little girl is walking to the playground. The weather is questionable, the clouds are forming, but she is insisting on going because they are to make crafts and then play on this day, according to a delightful story from Marilyn Ringle, Aledo, Ill.

Mother is concerned, but allows daughter to go to the playground. Suddenly, the wind whips and there is thunder and lightning. Mother hurries to the car to get her daughter.

As she drives to the edge of the playground, she spots her daughter. With each flash of lightning, the little girl is looking up and smiling.

Mom lowers the car window and shouts, "Hurry up. It's going to rain."

But the little girl repeatedly stops, and with each flash of lightning, tilts back her head and smiles.

"Why do you keeping stopping?" mom calls.

Daughter answers: "I am trying to look pretty. God keeps taking my picture."

❧

Trench coat belts:
An agony of winter

One of the most irritating problems of winter is the belt on the trench coat, followed in order by the lost gloves and the lost scarf.

There are world problems that never will be solved, and the trench coat belt, for sure, is one of them. Usually, the belt's tail end, the one with all the little holes, is as black as the old coal bin. It is covered with glop because men don't know what to do about the belts on their trench coats. When men get into cars, they slam the door and one end of the belt is left flapping along the street to gather up the goop of a sloppy winter.

"Frankly, I don't know what to do about this," says Jim Stopulos, the Davenport commercial real estate man. He is agonized and embarrassed to walk into Davenport's Outing Club with about 6 inches of his trench coat belt looking like it had been through the sewer.

"It's always dragging out my car door," he sighs. When Stopulos hangs up his coat, he is relieved to see that about a third of the other trench coats have similar grungy-looking tails on their belts.

"My best bet is to stick the tails into my pockets. I love trench coats, but hate to buckle myself into them," he says.

Most men are not the fastidious types and do not take the time to carefully straighten out belts and buckle them into the just-right grommet each time they put on their trench coat.

"It's a problem," says Greg Kautz, the Davenport clothier. "If you ignore the buckle, and knot the belt in front, it can twist and look very ratty."

It always looks ratty when I try to tie my trench coat belt because I am left-handed. Being a lefty, I can't even keep my shoes tied, which is a certain annoyance.

The first thing that some dapper fellows do when buying a new trench coat is to remove the belt and hide it someplace where they never will find it. That is well and good, but my wife complains when I do such a trick that those empty loops in the back look silly, as if I've lost my belt. Which I have, intentionally.

I'm convinced there is no way to really look sartorial with a belted trench coat.

"Tie it and it can look ratty. To buckle and unbuckle is tedious and time-consuming," Kautz says. "When we sell some trench coats, we double-band the belt in the back and leave it that way for life."

The sad, bad part is that trench coats belt are so silent. You never hear them clickity-clacking as you drive along from here to eternity.

As to lost gloves, that is another story. Some of us hapless ones can go through six pairs of gloves in a season. My wife insists she is going to put some little clippies, like for kids' mittens, on my sleeves.

As for scarves ... well, there is no solution.

ᏘᎭ

Worth Repeating

EVERY now and then, some tight-minded person will point out that I have written on the same subject in a surprisingly similar manner.

I will ask how many times that person has read Dickens' "A Christmas Carol" or heard Peter, Paul and Mary sing "Puff the Magic Dragon" or listened to Tony Bennett sing "I Left My Heart in San Francisco"?

For that matter, how many times have you had a lump in your throat when you heard Kate Smith sing, "God Bless America"? And how many times have you sung it yourself?

Well, here I go, repeating some of my favorites from the past 25 years.

Maybe some are familiar. Maybe some you forgot. Maybe some are just as well forgotten.

She took my seat!

Consider, for a trifle, this classic recited by the Rev. Bruce Antle at his Methodist church in Boca Grande, Fla., an island spa cherished by Quad-Citizens.

A parishioner's angry lament:

"A lady took my seat in church a while back. It's not that important, really. She's a very nice lady, kind and considerate. A good friend, in fact. There were several other seats available. I can sit anywhere. The people in our congregation are as friendly and caring as you will find anyplace in the world. A person should be comfortable sitting anyplace. It's no big deal.

"My seat is in the seventh row back from the front of the church. I'm sure she didn't intend to take my seat. She just wouldn't do that. Nor would anyone else in our fine church. It doesn't make that much difference.

"My seat is on the end of the pew, on the north side, by the windows. On your left as you come into the sanctuary. I can rest my left arm on the end of the pew. It's a good seat. I would never raise a fuss about a seat.

"I suppose she came early, and my seat appeared available. She probably didn't intend anything personal by taking my seat, but I would never raise a fuss about a seat or hold a grudge. There are several seats available on the south side. On your right as you come in I could have taken one of those. Those people who sit over there are very nice. Over there on the south side. I know most of those people. I would be welcome there, on the south side.

"Actually, it was about three months ago when she took my seat. I really don't know why she took it. I've never done anything to her. I've never taken her seat. I suppose I'll have to come an hour early now, to get my seat. Either that or sit on the south side.

"She really took it because it is one of the best seats in the house. That's why she took it. She had no business taking my seat. I wouldn't have been surprised if it had been a couple of other ladies in our church, who shall not remain unnamed. Donna Thege and Clarice Manstedt have been picking on me for a long time.

"I'm not going to sit on the south side. That's for south-siders. I'm a north-sider. I can just hear those south-siders if I sit over there. 'What's she doing over here?'

"I'll tell you what she's doing over here. Some unscrupulous person took her seat, that's what. She took it because it's the best seat in the house. And I'm not going to church two hours early to get what is rightfully mine from the beginning.

"This is the way great social injustices begin: Abusive people taking other people's seats in church. This is the way the seeds of revolution are sown. A person can only stand so much.

"Where is it going to end? If someone doesn't stand up and be counted, nobody's seat will be safe. People will just sit anyplace they please, and the next thing they'll do is to take my parking place, too. World order will be in shambles."

&

Turkey trot: You're right — those notes are back again!

If anything is indigenous to Davenport — besides being the birthplace of sliced bread and the site of the world's first appendectomy — it is the Turkey Note. Yep, yep, the Turkey Note, spelled with caps, because no place but Davenport claims to be the home of the Turkey Note.

When a *Quad-City Times* photographer was assigned to photograph the class of Diane Stensrud making Turkey Notes at Eisenhower School, Davenport, he was puzzled and asked, "What the heck is a Turkey Note?"

Each year at Thanksgiving, the Davenport Public Library is asked about Turkey Notes. There are queries from all over. Once, for a piece on folklore, even the lofty American Heritage magazine called me for an explanation of Turkey Notes.

Innocent newcomers and strangers to Davenport ask, "What are they?" Only Davenport. No place else.

Do they ask about Turkey Notes in Billings, Mont.?

Of course not.

Do they ask about Turkey Notes in Newport, R.I.?

Har-de-har-har. You think those effete Easterners ever heard of, or care about, Turkey Notes? Only Davenporters love turkey notes.

Let's hope Turkey Notes never disappear. They are akin to a heart on a Valentine. They are four lines of verse, wrapped tube-like in colored paper with fringy edges, and put on the dinner plate at Thanksgiving or handed to mom and dad or classmates. The meter doesn't matter. It does not have to follow a da-da-da, da-da-da rhythm of a Burma Shave sign. All that's necessary is for every line to begin with the word "turkey."

From what anyone can believe, Germans brought the Turkey Note folly to

Davenport from Schleswig-Holstein. Most of the Germans who populated Davenport came from Schleswig-Holstein, so it could be imagined they brought Turkey Notes with them. But then again, why were the Germans having Thanksgiving turkey? That's an American holiday. By way of mention, has anyone ever heard of the Swedes or the Belgians in Moline going for Turkey Note lolly-gagging?

Researching Turkey Notes, the Davenport Library found mention of them in an old Democrat & Leader column called "Homemade Hooch," by Bob Feeney. Feeney thoughtfully wrote: "It seems to me that the topic of Turkey Notes would make an interesting subject for some university student working for a master's degree. I toss out the idea free of charge to any student."

Lots of Turkey Notes have been made through the years. Those notes from Mrs. Stensrud's students at Eisenhower are a lot cooler than any I remember:

Turkey black,
Turkey pink,
Turkey says,
Give me a wink.
— *Brandon Kuhrt*

Turkey bones,
Turkey feet,
Turkey says,
Just eat the meat.
— *David Whalen*

Turkey five,
Turkey six,
Turkey's tired,
He ran the Bix.
— *Mitchell Jahns*

Turkey black,
Turkey white,
Wundram's column
is out of sight!
— *Ashley Bittner* (a most
perceptive, bright young woman)

ॐ

Two olives, please; the martini is back

During a party for his third attempt at retirement, ex-officio banker Tom Otting lamented that a human being no longer can get a martini, straight-up.

"Up" is pure, iced in a shaker the moment before and served in a dewy-stemmed glass.

"It's the true way to go," we chimed, lamenting that the martini is becoming too urbanized or yuppy-fied or civilized to be called a true "martin."

"Martin" is the way aficionados prefer to celebrate the classic drink that was the choice of Franklin D. Roosevelt, Winston Churchill, Frank Sinatra, Jack London, Ernest Hemingway and W.C. Fields.

Too many people today prefer their martinis be served on the rocks, in a squat glass, which defeats the whole purpose of the sophisticated drink.

They also desecrate the drink by having a preference for vodka instead of gin. *Real* martini drinkers tolerate only gin.

"Beefeater gin martini, up wit' an olive. No twist, right?" the bartender must repeat.

Straight up, with a rivulet trickling like a maiden's tear down the side of a stemmed glass. Always, two olives. Once, Sinatra was asked:

"Would you like an onion in your martini, Mr. Sinatra?"

Sinatra's snarling reply: "Listen, pal ... this is a drink, not a salad."

The martini was offish for a decade or so, but now it is coming back strong.

"It's our most requested drink," says Amy Kissock, a bartender at McKinley's, a long-ago Clinton lumberyard office that has been restored into a classy restaurant/bar.

"I like my martini up and dirty," she says. That means up in a stemmed glass. "Up and dirty" is to add a tiny bit of olive juice in lieu of vermouth.

The first savage martini called for mostly vermouth, an affront to the gin.

Prohibition days, and their alleged bathtub gin, had a norm of four swigs of gin to one swig of vermouth. After World War II, Stan Wiedner ordained they be 10-to-1 at his Plantation restaurant in Moline. Nic Chirekos tempered that to 5-to-1, which is as close to perfection as possible.

The ultimate martini is the work of an artist who carefully stacks the ice in a shaker. George Bush, a long-time barkeep in Fulton, Ill., had a perfect understanding with the martini. He was convinced that gin could be bruised if not handled with care. The gin must smoke, or steam, when poured onto the ice from a height of 12 inches, always a generous 4 ounces per drink.

Those of us who comprehend the martini are pleased that this icon of American culture has once again found its way to the fore. According to the late, great noospaper columnist, H.L. Mencken, the martini is "The only American invention as perfect as a sonnet." James Bond requires that his be shaken, not stirred, and travel book author Barnaby Conrad III finds it a "Nostalgic passport to another era ... when women were either ladies or dames, men wore hats and deals were done with a handshake."

The martini has found its way into every aspect of American culture, from film (Nic and Nora in "The Thin Man") to F. Scott Fitzgerald's "The Great Gatsby."

I confess to having experimented with this wanton form of self-indulgence.

With Jack Sundine, then publisher of the Moline Dispatch, I once searched for the perfect martini. In lieu of vermouth, we tried light amounts of Amana rhubarb wine. It was a vulgar drink. With a doctor friend, I experimented with an Italian import, strawberry vermouth. It was another disaster.

There are certain ground rules for martinis. It is not a table drink and does not mix well with cocktail party chit-chat. It should be absorbed while sitting at a bar, which preferably, has soft piano music.

And who knows, perhaps a lovely woman with silken shoulders will appear. She will pluck an olive from your glass and ask, "What's new, how is the world treating you ...?"

༄

Gin and raisins for what ails you

I have been accused of always writing about home remedies, such as warm goose grease for chest colds and Sloan's Liniment and sugar for sore throat.

In my wanderings, I have encountered any number of successful kitchen ointments, but consuming gin-soaked raisins to cure arthritis may be the most widely publicized of our time.

"It is the craziest thing," said Al Hallene Sr., Moline, who may have been the messenger to launch the "curative" process to the afflicted millions.

Paul Harvey, of "the rest of the story" fame, has talked about it on the airwaves, and the cure has been repeated at every crossroads junction general store and at every bridge club.

Let's start at the beginning.

One day, Hallene said, he and a Moline dentist were golfing. The dentist complained of arthritis in his hand. Hallene offered sympathy and said he had the same thing.

There was an interchange of how they had heard about a strange gin-and-raisin recipe for relief. It was said to come not from a rattle-shaking witch doctor but by way of a physician in the eastern United States.

Before going on any more, the formula: Buy a box of golden raisins and spread them out in a glass — not tin — pie plate. Plastic might work, but glass is best.

Then, buy a fifth of the cheapest gin you can find. Pour it onto the golden raisins scattered in the pie pan. Let the whole works marinate for exactly seven days. After a week, the raisins have absorbed all the gin. No gin should be left. Those raisins are bloated like Iowa pigs at the slop trough.

Now, the fun begins, if you have arthritis. You eat nine of those gin-sated raisins a day. There will be a lot of them, so you'd best seal them in a jar so they don't dry out. If you're lucky, by the time you are finished with all the raisins, your arthritis pain will be relieved.

The celebrated gin-and-raisin cure came to attention during a meeting of the highly respected MacArthur Foundation in Chicago. Al Hallene was a director of this organization, likely the most philanthropic group in America, and one of the great benefactors of PBS. One board member was severely afflicted with arthritis and Hallene casually mentioned that — as a long shot — he might try the treatment.

At the time, sufferer could barely shake hands. At the next meeting, his condition was notably improved. "Say, that stuff really works," he said, congratulating Hallene. Across the table that day was Paul Harvey, also a director of the MacArthur Foundation. "Paul Harvey's rabbit ears flopped up, and it wasn't long until he had the arthritis formula of gin and raisins on the air," Hallene said.

There is more. At another meeting of the MacArthur Foundation, a director said he wasn't sure if he was to eat nine raisins a day or drink nine shots of gin a day, so he did both and had never felt better.

Spray away your pains

It did seem an odd coincidence that Eldon Baxter of Davenport should wander into the office on the eve of Pearl Harbor with a spray can of WD40.

Eldon, one of those who survived Pearl Harbor on that day of infamy — December 7, 1941 — was debunking the infamous gin-and-raisin recipe.

"This WD40 stuff is the best for arthritis," said Eldon, showing how he sprayed the lubricant on his knees and elbows.

Others have repeated to me that WD40 really works for aches and pains of the joints. Thank goodness I don't need it, but if I did, I'd take the gin-and-raisin formula any day. Extra dry, with an olive and twist.

છ

Purely Personal

IF I write of myself, and my experiences, and my family, that's the way I feel. I write — for better or worse — what is in me.

Wives are fair game for a columnist, but children can be touchy so I generally steer clear of them.

My suffering wife is a target, like the time she dropped me off at Shannon's restaurant to pick up some hard rolls for supper while she drove around the block. In my simple mind, I forgot that she was going 'round and 'round and sat down to knock off a chicken pot pie. I was sucking my teeth, asking about cake, when she parked and came inside. "I've been around the block at least 20 times? Did you forget about me?"

Sometimes, I've written of personal tragedy.

Still, purely personal "is me" — and so may it be!

Amen.

Home alone

It must be time to make the bed because I can't find the TV remote

I looked at my mysteriously blue-speckled shorts and undershirts, just out of the washer, and decided that man was not meant to live alone.

My wife had suggested that while I toiled the winter away, she would go to Florida for a couple months. Fine.

She deserved the rest and the warmth.

Man was not meant to live alone

Everything about the house is a mystery to me, including the MidAmerican energy bill, which is twice as high as it usually is, even though I am away from home most of the time and keep the temp set at a cool 66.

I talk to my wife often, but it wasn't until she had been in Florida a month that she thought to ask if I was changing the bed every Saturday, which is her ritual.

She was stunned to learn that not only had I not changed the bed since she left, I had not made the bed in a month.

"You mean you go to bed at night in a bed that hasn't been made?"

It didn't bother me to reply that I never thought it necessary to make a bed.

"I just make a little nest and crawl under the covers," I told her.

(I might have to make it today, though, because in all that rumple I have lost the button-thing to change the TV, which I doze to sleep by.)

Man was not meant to live alone

My wife had given me instructions, to which I paid no attention, for operating the washing machine and the dishwasher. After my first batch of undershirts and shorts and socks came up speckled with blue detergent, I casually gave her a call and asked what I had done wrong.

She is an understanding person and reminded me that the detergent should go into the bottom first, and the clothes put on top. I had done the opposite, sprinkling the detergent on top of my shorts; hence, the polka-dot effect.

Also, I never before believed this, but I now know it is God's truth that washers and dryers do eat socks. I have four mismatches. Oh, fiddle-dee-dee.

I just threw them away, never expecting to find their mates.

Man was not meant to live alone

"Are you eating properly?" my wife asked one night.

Well, yes, after a fashion. Usually, I find baloney on rye, with a tall glass of ice tea, just right for breakfast. At noon, I eat no lunch.

Sometimes at night, I have a late supper of another baloney sandwich and for dessert, peach halves, which I keep (still in the can) in the fridge.

Dishes have been a genuine problem. I could not figure out the dishwasher, and had run out of dishes. I did the unthinkable, something that gave my wife the shakes upon my mention of it. I ventured one night that I had turned over dirty plates and eaten on the other side. That was only temporary, and I am elated to report that I have conquered operation of the dishwasher, but still am mystified by buttons that say "cool dry" and "warm dry" and "pans only."

Pans are no worry, though, because I don't use them. I hate pans. Pans are impossible to clean, except for soup. The man who would create a better pan would make a million, a disposable pan that would be tossed out after one use, just like a paper plate.

Man was not meant to live alone

Getting back to the bed ... I shall make it this morning. By now, I admit, it's kind of a mess to crawl into an unmade bed.

Worse than that, though, is to crawl into bed without someone to snuggle up to on a cold night.

Man was not meant to live alone ... at least, not this man

ও

Sleepless on the wrong side of the bed

Here I toss at midnight, trying to get some sleep. I blame Jay Leno. Maybe I am just accustomed to going to sleep half-watching "M*A*S*H," which doesn't come on now until 11:30. I yearn for Johnny Carson. I could always go to sleep when the Carson show was on.

Leno, on the other hand or the other side, is not the reason at all. It is because I have moved to the other side of the bed. I am asking my brain and body to move from my life-long left side of the bed to the right side of the bed and my brain and body are resisting.

It is akin to the movie, "Sleepless in Seattle."

I think of this at 2 or 3 a.m. I find myself watching the Home Shopping Network, but even that cannot put me to sleep. It's impossible to watch late-night TV without being hammered with all those commercials about fat abs and glutes. Abs and glutes. They keep me awake.

"Flatten your abs or glutes in weeks with our new Miracle Muscle Machine, only $19.95 a month for 90 months."

In all these loving years of marriage, I have gone to sleep with my wife approximately 15,320 times, curled up on the left side of the bed. Now I am switched because the left side of the bed is closer to her bathroom, and I am called upon to sleep on the right side of the bed.

My body and soul don't like the move one bit. Everything is changed. Even the sheets on the right-hand side feel different. The covers do not come up around me the way they used to when I slept on the left side of the bed. I have the same pillows, but the bed feels dissimilar and the pillows feel flatter. I know they are flatter, and the TV remote control — which I usually could find without fumbling — is utterly elusive.

My wife sleeps beside me, but now she is on the left side of the bed. She notices my restive sleep but says my being on the right side has given her more rest. When I slept on the left, I would regularly toss a right arm on her slumbering form. Then, in my sleep, I would dream that I was typing a column and regularly tap my fingers on her shoulder or back or side.

"You must have a long column," she would sleepily protest.

In my palmy days, when playing a cornet (very badly, I might add) I would dream of being on the Aragon or Trianon bandstand, and while asleep, would work the three horn valve fingers of my right hand on my wife's shoulder in some intricate cadenza of "The Carnival of Venice." Both of these habits were always disconcerting for my wife who would awaken while I snored.

I stare, sleepless in the dim night. It is the same overheard ceiling fan, but that is no comfort. The view from the right side of the bed has changed, though, which may be part of my problem. No longer do I look upon an etagere with doo-dads and framed photos of grandkids. Now, I look out at evergreen trees, rimmed by a quite soft-overhead-ish street light. That should be calming, their boughs bowed in snow, but it isn't.

My sleeplessness has to be caused because I am sleeping on the wrong side of the bed.

In quiet desperation I turned to Carol Everson, who runs the Sleep Center at Genesis Medical Center, Davenport. She pointed out that couples usually sleep on the same side of the bed wherever they go, such as motels or visiting in the home of others.

"We're creatures of habit; habits are hard to change, but I think you'll get used to it, and it won't affect your psyche," she said.

I'm not sure. I'm still worried about all those abs and glutes.

૨઼

Moving is plain hell!

The terror, pains and the few joys of getting from here to somewhere

We are moving today. Everything is taped into about 800 boxes and the furniture is in neat rows, waiting for the van. My back pains. I'm not sure if I am dead or belong in a straitjacket.

Moving is hell!!! (Three exclamation points.) Some people buy a house and stay there all their lives. The more I think of it, that is not a bad idea.

We have a habit of moving because we love houses. We like to work with them. This will be our sixth house. This move will be our last move, my wife says.

I am not sure. I want to some day build a house on a lake, a picturesque place that looks like a lighthouse. I'm serious.

The only solace I can find in this particular move is that I will not pull the absurd blunder I pulled when we moved to Pleasant Valley and I had packed all the clothes in long boxes. One side was to go to the new house, the other side to the Salvation Army. Confused, I gave all my wife's summer wardrobe to the Salvation Army. Her psyche is still not the same.

For weeks now, we have been packing. The movers, checking the load, said they never had seen so many boxes. That is because we have so many memories.

One does not throw away the love and memories of 46 years of marriage without boxes and boxes of sweet sentiment.

How could anyone toss out the funny rubber-banana nose that Red Skelton gave me? How can we throw away the cards from our wedding gifts, or the little bead bracelets worn when our kids were born? How can I throw away the note that our son, Peter, left on the calendar of Jan. 1, 1977, when we were at a New Year's Eve party:

"My friend Gary made it home all right. His dad came to pick him up about

1:15 a.m. We played Monopoly until falling asleep. Happy New Year, mom and dad. Love, Peter." (I remember, one of his young chums had come to spend New Year's Eve with him.)

My wife no longer saves bows from gift packages, but she does save little empty boxes. I save everything. All things, such as one of those little lights that you once lit to get a server's attention at Bishop's. And big things, like a full-size wooden merry-go-round horse and a Ferris wheel seat. Shouldn't everyone have a carousel horse and a Ferris wheel seat?

Being a sentimental sap, I save everything ever written to me ... a sweet note from a grandson: "Grandpa Bill was the best singer of happy birthday to my dad," or a letter from my idol, Herb Caen, the late, lamented San Francisco columnist, praising a humble piece I had written.

Well, we're poised to move today. A house has a soul, as certain as a human being, and with it will be a blubbery emotion when I speak farewell to our home built into a Bettendorf hillside.

One last time this morning, before we move, I will stretch out in our bed — as I have every morning for eight years — and stare out the window toward a crook in the limb of an oak tree that must have been there when Columbus landed.

My wife will ask, as she often has: "What are you staring at?"

"My secret," I always said. "Everyone should have secrets."

Today, I shall share that secret with her. In the top of the oak tree is a fork in a limb that brought back my childhood.

Someday, I always vowed, I would have a tree trimmer go up there and cut it down for me. The limb would have made the perfect slingshot.

Anyway, with sentimental memories, au revoir, to our sprawling old house that long ago entertained film stars like Alice Faye and bandleader Phil Harris, and once, the whole White Sox ball team.

Chapter 6 begins today ... life in a villa. Well, that's just a fancy name for what I call a condo.

જ

We never ate supper until the money was counted

Future reference; Snap. Click. What image do I have of my dad? It's a hot summery night, the Emerson electric fan is oscillating from the top of the refrigerator because only movie theaters were air conditioned in that day and age. Dad is at the kitchen table, in a necktie, a little after 9 p.m., counting the day's receipts from our grocery store.

We never ate supper until after the store closed and the money was counted.

He ruled the roost, and his meal could not settle unless he knew that the cash register and the pay-outs tallied.

Others turn their fancy on Father's Day to glazed memories of fishing or man-to-man talks with good old dad. Some recall endlessly tossing a softball, back and forth, back and forth, in the back yard. That's the picture you're supposed to get, kid. Well, my dad was different, bless his young heart, for he died too young, always too busy — in search of that elusive rainbow that too often slipped through his fingers. We had too little time to play. He worked too hard.

"Some day, we'll all take a vacation," he would say. We never did, because there never was time. He was the most ambitious, hard-working dreamer I ever have known.

But did I know him? Not really. He was always too busy. It's my fault. I should have made time to know him. As the years slip so swiftly away, don't all of us wonder and wish, "Had I only known my dad better."

If there is any moral in all of this, take time for dad. John Marquand once wrote a best-seller, "So Little Time." Don't let there be so little time that none is left for you to get to know your dad.

Certainly, my dad was a personality. So many careers, a few small fortunes lost and won, a man driven to achieve. The Depression-bred were that way. "A dollar is your best friend; find out how many friends you have when you don't have one," he'd drone into my young ears. He was full of homilies like that. Another: "It doesn't cost a nickel to say 'hello' to everyone."

When young, he drifted into the newspaper biz. He was a gifted copywriter who sidelined with some ad agencies and toiled his way to becoming ad manager of the old Democrat & Leader. After a small lifetime, 24 years, he got into a snit with the management and quit to make it on his own. His timing was off. He had prospered in his job, but had invested heavily in Cities Service stock. He lost his shirt in the crash of Black Friday. His sympathetic old pal, Mel Foster Sr., was peddling footwear at the Tradehome Shoe Store in downtown Davenport at the time. He suggested: "Let's go into the real estate business together." Well, one of them did.

In the most dismal of days of the Great Depression, my dad opened a grocery store. People had more fortitude then. When everyone else was failing, he made money the old-fashioned way. His ads read: "The best in the West — fancy groceries and quality meats. Cold meat sandwiches, five cents to eight cents, for less than you can make them at home. Cold ginger ale. Ice cream cones, five cents, three for a dime. A block of ice free with every 50 cent picnic purchase. Open from 7 a.m. to 9 p.m., seven days a week."

In my graying years, I wonder about this driven man. What made him tick?

How I wish I could visit with my dad today, to wonder of his dreams. When I was growing up, no one as "old" as my dad could possibly have had dreams and wishes and hopes, could they? My old eyes dream, and I conjure up a vision of him always dressed up. He even mowed the lawn in a dress shirt and tie. His was not the sloppily dressed generation.

Well, he wisely quit the corner grocery store, which grew to be quite a big, profitable store, after 10 years. A good time to get out: the dawn of the supermarket age. He switched to buying and selling farms, making a buck here, losing a buck there, always meticulous in his honesty. Not often was he "stuck," but I particularly remember how he envisioned that postwar farmers would be starved for farm equipment. He bought the first two flat cars of corn pickers off the line of some fly-by-night company that quickly faded into bankruptcy. Before he could sell the pickers, he discovered that none had driveshafts.

Life was like that for him. Ups and downs and ups. He whistled a lot. He liked to whistle, "Life is Just a Bowl of Cherries." He used to tell me, "The best you can get from life is an even break." But the Big C did not give him his even break. He died, barely over the age of 60.

I never thought of him a great deal when I was young. He was always so busy. Or, more likely, no excuses, I was always too busy. Now, I miss him so much.

I wish that we could talk. I wish I could hear him whistle "Life is Just a Bowl of Cherries" just once more.

❧

Thoughts on dining

Why, at the precise moment when you have a mouthful of food, does the waitress/waiter always ask, "How are things going for you? Can I get you anything?" How does one courteously answer when you have a mouthful of meatloaf?

Are you suspicious, too, when the person waiting on you says, "Good choice." Then, you hear him or her say the same thing to the person in the next booth who has ordered something entirely different.

No restaurateur has ever satisfactorily explained why servers are so quick to take your order, but so slow in bringing your check.

I wonder what they do with the bread or rolls that are left over in my bread basket?

When I am microwaving something so simple as a Chinese dinner, why must I have to look at the directions on the box at least 10 times? And why are the directions hidden, and printed in 4-point type, which is smaller than the classified ads?

If I am in a restaurant, I get myself all worked up over what the person next to me is eating. That taco salad looks so much better than the dab of chicken salad I got in a stuffed tomato. It must be some crazy syndrome, but I cannot enjoy my meal, worrying that I should have ordered what the other person did.

Why is it — about half the time — the person who arrived in the restaurant later than me has soup or salad before I even get my silverware and napkin?

Why have food manufacturers never packaged the greatest kid-treat of all time, graham crackers with frosting?

Why are so many restaurants becoming such echo chambers that you can't carry on a conversation?

əۥ

My graduation speech
no one will hear ...

Every now and then, some school asks me to give a graduation speech. Mostly, I'm not asked back because I don't exactly give an orthodox address. That is, no school except Hamilton Tech. I have given so many commencement speeches there that they have given me an honorary degree in electronic engineering, which has been no help whatsoever in hooking up my VCR.

Still, I like to give commencement speeches, mostly high school, and update them all the time. This is my 2001 version, one that no one asked me to give ...

Most graduation speeches tackle the big connection, but I would like to pass along a poor man's gems of wisdom for getting along in Quad-City Land, good advice, like never retell the plot of movies like "The Mummy Returns," or never believe that you know everything, or try to be at peace with everyone, even rude jerks.

Very often, kids, life is like a warm can of Pepsi out of a pop machine on a hot day. It's not what you expected. I advise you to ignore the breaks, because you will probably get more good breaks than bad ones. That is, unless you are betting that the Cubs will win the pennant, no matter how miraculously well they're doing so far this season.

I advise you to not worry about every little thing and begin to enjoy life.

Long ago, as a punk doing obits, my desk was near Bob Feeney, a competent, jovial reporter who always told me not to worry so much. Though still an inveterate worrier, I am often consoled by Feeney's advice: "Listen, kid, most problems will solve themselves."

Once, in writing about advice that fathers give their sons, I quoted Bill Davis, Scott County Attorney, who recalled the best counsel his dad ever gave him: "Don't worry about the nickel-and-dime stuff."

In other words, unless it's a big-time concern, this, too, will pass.

Life is full of delights, so enjoy them now while you are as young as springtime.

Enjoy music. When John Bernatz, retiring band director at Davenport Central High, took the baton for his last concert, he made a plea to the kids:

"Stay with music, performing or listening, all your life — you will be enriched."

If you don't already, follow the magic sounds of Mozart and Vivaldi and Liszt and even the bombastic John Philip Sousa. And love the joy of jazz, the indefinable sounds of Bix, the spirit of Satchmo and bop-cheeked Dizzy Gillespie. Try Tony Bennett some time instead of Kid Rock.

Always be a gentleman, always be a lady. Open doors for everyone, bum or banker. Kids, you probably never heard of the comic legend Red Skelton, who said he acted like a gentleman for so long that he became one. See the world as a friend. Smile at the weary person working late at night at the supermarket checkout counter.

Have a love for animals. Staring into a dog's eyes will draw out a mystery as deep as God, and ask nothing in return but your love. Always remember, God spelled backwards is dog.

Oh, I have plenty of other pithy advice for you grads:

Remember, you can always find enough nickels and dimes on the floor of your car to buy a package of Twinkies.

Eat less broccoli and more Whitey's malts, chocolate preferred.

Take time to sniff more flowers, watch more sunsets and spend your spare change riding Ferris wheels.

The best way to bake potatoes is in a pile of burning autumn leaves, that is if the law allows you to burn leaves.

Girls, don't date men who smell too pretty. Be certain that Old Spice can cover up a multitude of personality disorders.

When you get your diploma, take it home to your mom or dad or whoever has seen you this far through life. Hug them and say, "This is for you, for loving me and putting up with me and for driving me to all the soccer practices and marching band rehearsals."

When you go off to college, and I hope you do, call your grandma once a week. She may be so thrilled that she will send you some of her oatmeal cookies.

❧

Lost domains:
The all-guy barbershop

So this is Saturday, a day when guys always used to get their hair cut — by other men. Every time I get my hair cut, I wonder where all the male barbers have gone.

Once, there was a barbershop on every corner of the Quad-Cities. I mean real he-man places that reeked of Lucky Tiger and had hair all over the floor. It's different now. Most barbers are women. And come to mention, when was the last time you saw a striped pole outside a barbershop?

"Women have really taken over in the all-male barbershop," says Ron Gottschalk, who gave up the shears after 41 years. His shop was in Bettendorf, and he reasons that at one time or another he cut the hair of every man and boy in the city. Women are good barbers, he says, but there is a difference.

"Oh, I can tell when a woman has cut a man's hair. The back side is blocked off, instead of using shears. I watched the inauguration of President Bush. All those men had blocked-off backs. I bet women cut their hair."

I confess, as must a lot of men, that I don't go to a he-man barber shop. I wonder how many of them exist, though I know they do. I go to a place where my hair is cut by Rita, who always wafts of some delicious essence like Clinique Happy.

Still, I miss the odor of talcum, the swish of the barber's brush, and his question, "Want some tonic?" Or to be splashed on the face with Mennen's aftershave that smarted all the way back to the office.

Lots of times, I feel like a wimp when I enter my barbershop, which really is a beauty salon. Every now and then, a guy or two is there, but they are much younger and want the stylish look that only beauticians seem to handle.

When I wait my turn, I am embarrassed to pick up the magazines. Usually, there are stacks of Vogue or Cosmopolitan. The magazines I remember from the good old barbershops were Sports Afield or maybe — in the later racier years — Playboy.

Oh, it's not that I dislike going to a beauty parlor to get my hair cut. It's just that I feel out of place in a flimsy chair with chrome arms, when I can remember those icebox-size Kocher porcelain chairs with the pump handle. You walked out smelling good and feeling fine because the barber usually massaged your head. It was your choice if you wanted regular brilliantine or that spiffy stuff, sloshed out of a tall-necked bottle, called Vitalis.

Maybe we lost all of that when moms began taking their little boys for haircuts. They didn't want to malinger in those male asylums and took them to their own beauty parlors.

Most gray hairs remember the palatial hotel barbershops, like the six-chair shop at the Fort Armstrong in Rock Island, or the shop, with tiled walls the color of sweet cream, at the Mississippi Hotel, Davenport. Barbers like Kermit Sutton had chairs there, along with Lou Smutzer. A manicurist named Lucille burnished nails and Neil O'Neil, shined shoes. Neil used to be a barber, but gave it up after wrecking his scissors hand with an ax while cutting off a chicken's head.

Those were the years of the traveling salesman, who lived with a smile and a shoeshine and a barbershop shave (usually at the hotel) every morning. A shave was 35 cents.

A good barber like Smutzer always had good stories, too, like the time in the Blackhawk Hotel's big six-chair shop when he trimmed the hair of a burly customer. He didn't know who it was until the fellow gave him a light tap on the chin. "Now, you can say you were hit by Jack Dempsey."

Well, the corner barbershop that dads and grandpas remember is disappearing fast. So what, I suppose. The young guys are happy with the $15 (on up) female stylists.

Still, I miss the good old barbershop. They were great debating parlors. If we had them, there would be no need for Larry King or "Nightline" or "Meet the Press." Everything would be solved over the Vitalis.

❧

In defense of men
who wear bow ties

Lately, I have taken to wearing bow ties. I've spent most of my life wearing long, regular ties, using only a Windsor knot with a dimple in the center.

It is OK to put Windsor in capital letters because it's commonly said that the knot was invented by Edward VIII, the Duke of Windsor, the one who abdicated the throne of England for the woman he loved.

But now, I have accepted the bow tie. It may not be for everyone, but I claim it works for me. If it makes me look a little odd, rather clownish, that suits me just fine. I like clowns.

Gentleman's Quarterly, the magazine of style, once said that men who wore bow ties were fops. Now, who is to say locals — nonetheless than Dudley "Dudes" Priester, the eminent contractor who goes for the diamond-type bow, and Pieter Hanson, the banker — are fops because they wear bow ties. Jim Victor, the financier, is testing the bow tie envelope. You see him out and about and on the telly in a classic, conservative bow tie.

If all of us are fops, so goes Winston Churchill and Paul Simon, the former U.S. senator from Illinois, who claims to own more than 200 bow ties. Also, my dad, who even mowed the lawn wearing a neat small pattern polka dot blue and white bow tie because it made him look noteworthy.

They say that he-men don't wear bow ties. I don't go for that, though at the Gentry Shop in Davenport they philosophically say, "You either go for them or you don't. Some men won't even go near them."

The truth is, most men snub bow ties because they don't know how to tie one. Otherwise, they would wear them because you look distinguished and can't spill soup on a bow tie. Wearing a bow tie is a sign of a headstrong man and shows individuality, that you are confident enough in yourself to wear them.

I learned the art of fashioning a bow tie at the knees (that's correct, knees) of the late William Scott, a folksy judge in Scott County district court. He illustrated the craft by tying a bow tie over his knee, and instructed me to practice the same on my own knee. Though a built-in fumbler, I caught on quickly. It's all in the thumb in the last little hole.

"Once you learn how to tie a bow tie, you never forget. It's like riding a bicycle," says Hanson, the banker. "They're even easier to tie when you're running late in the morning."

You can tell in an instant a hand-tied bow from one of those inane clip-ons, which are an insult to manly humanity. No bow tie should ever be perfect.

I recall many bow tie stories. Once, at a wedding reception at the Outing Club, the father of the bride's bow tie went askew and he needed help in retying it. I watched the goings-on as he asked the late Urban Ott, a mortician, for assistance. Exasperated, Ott seriously said, "Stretch out on the floor — I can only tie a bow if the subject is flat on his back."

Then, there was that long-ago time in my lettuce days (being very green) I showed up in the newsroom in a bow tie. An executive growled, pulled on one end of the tie and untied it.

"The only person who can wear a bow tie is the CEO of this corporation, and that's *not* you."

It was better to work on the copy desk than going on the road as an abdominal truss salesman, so I took it off. I suppose that was opportune, because I'm still here, and wearing bow ties nearly every day.

ন্ধ

All is calm: Sing a song of Christmas

Now they have all gone, and the house is very still.

It is Christmas Eve. For the first time this evening, I hear the familiar sound of the December wind blustering and flustering around our house.

No more house, really; now our life is a condo, but that is the way of change, not to mention heartbreaking joy.

The December winds no longer knock at a shutter, but now make "pssst" whistling sounds through a sliding door. I remember it once swept snow across our long-ago home's brick dooryard.

But here in my little den, under the soft reading lamp, it is warm and still.

My wife asks to close the glass doors of the fireplace; no, I want them open, to see the coals fade as she goes to bed on this quietest of Christmases — for our children all are gone now.

The nest is empty. They have all gone now.

With some melancholy, I stare at those fond ornaments on the tree ... the little bauble that Peter made while in the Jefferson School chorus in 1971; Becky's first-grade hand imprint; Tim's little orange clay ornament, with childish letters — "To my mom and dad, 1961."

But such is life, and this is Christmas, a boundless privilege. Life is a series of ribboned packages and would not be worth taking were it not for all its surprises.

Was it not Einstein who said, "Only a life lived for others is a life worthwhile?" Christmas is a time for such quiet thoughts, of life and love and stars and dark skies.

The parting voice of my preacher, Rev. Al VanderMeer, still booms in my ears from the Christmas Eve services: "The deepest need that people have is for love — (1) from God, (2) from other people."

Preacher Al and I had been talking of life and living it for others, and spoke of a good friend who is ever-so-slowly dying of cancer on this Christmas. One side of her hospital room is a wallpaper of Christmas cards.

Two women, during a visit, did her nails to cheer her sad heart.

Next door, another woman lay dying, also of cancer, in a room barren of even the simplest of poinsettias and not a visitor.

It was Christmas, but for both of these, it did not seem right to die.

Perhaps the bells will wait.

I stretch in my recliner, listening to the sound of this night that is as soft as candlelight. I think of others in other homes, wedging the Christmas tree until it stands straight, welcoming family weary from the road, wrapping the final round of presents.

Earlier in the day, I looked at Christmas tree lots. Most all trees were sold, and the ones left went cheap. There is no sadder sight than a Christmas tree lot on Christmas Eve night, with the scraggly leftovers so lonely — never to feel a bauble or bangle or to hear the wonder of a child's Christmas morning.

But merrily, dreaming at my fireplace, I turn up a tape of Mannheim Steamroller Christmas — harpsichord, toy piano, dulcimer, and wonder if we expect too much of Christmas. We try to jam into it the forgotten kindliness and humanity of the whole year.

I listened to a foot-weary salesperson, Betty Houston, say yesterday, "It's all too much at once."

I agree. I like to take my Christmas a little at a time, and thus I drift along into the holidays and let them overtake me unexpectedly.

I like to wake up some fine morning like this, after falling asleep in the chair last night, and say:

"Why, this is Christmas Day!"

ൠ

'Tis the day after Christmas ...

... and still those fearsome words echo: 'Assembly required'

"I'll take this bookcase," I told the young salesperson at the Quad-City store. It was a dandy price, only $99.

"No," she said. "You can't have it. You'll have to take the one in the box and assemble it yourself."

I couldn't even lift the box without a certain hernia and asked if it might be delivered.

"That'll be $25," the clerk said.

Worried, I asked if it could be assembled for me.

"That will be another $35," she said.

Already, it would be more than half the purchase price just to get this confounded bookcase put together and into my den. I opted for delivery, and figured that even my monkey mind could assemble anything so simple as a bookcase.

Thus began the nightmare that all of us have faced, one time or another: "Assembly required."

What shocked me down to the socks was the 12-page instruction folio, with a warning on the very front, "Do not contact store for parts or assembly assistance." It was suggested that I call a toll-free number if I had problems.

No question, there would be problems. In the carton was a plastic sack with about five pounds of screws and bolts and brackets. The mystic hardware included such names as hex head screws, Phillips head screws, mending plates, cam studs, plastic l-brackets, cam housings, wooden dowels, locking shelf pins and simple nails.

Also frightening was the notice: "For reasons of manufacturing efficiencies, you may find extra hardware and unused holes in the parts." Come on, now. What kind of talk is that?

Still, I was assured by Step No. 1: "This furniture is easy to put together. Just follow these step-by-step instructions." Only a hammer and a couple screwdrivers and a hex wrench (what's that?) would be needed.

Ha! What a joke. If I could assemble this mess, I could build a space station. Needless to say (so why say it?) the whole thing left me totally boggled.

Every now and then my wife would check. She would find me clutching a handful of hex screws and moaning piteously.

The instructions were not meant for clucks. "Make sure all the housings are in their open position by pointing the arrow of the cam housings toward the holes in the edge."

Huh?

Well, my bookcase is assembled. It is handsome, with the encyclopedias in place and plants on the shelves.

But don't give me any credit for this feat. By midnight I gave up. I called in a professional carpenter. Next day, it only took him two hours, but he admitted, "It was a little tricky."

❧

Savvy with the supermarket sack

Artfully arranged, with a celery 'bouquet' at the top,
it was a sense of peaceful order

At the supermarket the other day, a lackadaisical young man was plopping my purchases into one plastic bag after another. The sacks were slippery, which made it easy for him to slide the celery alongside the cereal box.

I cringed, because packing a grocery bag is a fine art.

Speaking from long practice and experience, I question the abilities of today's supermarket baggers. Now, don't get me wrong; most of you try, but you just don't have the finesse that I grew up with. I spent my young years in the family grocery store, and my ears still ring with papa's strong words:

"A grocery bag can be beautiful."

He was an artist of sorts, who used chalky stuff to paint bargains of the day on his windows. He underlined prices with squiggles or dolled up bargains with (of all things) winging birds.

But grocery bags were his specialty. Beautiful, yes. It can be a practical-packed square bag, too, that fits comfortably under your arm. It's all in the packing, and the well-meaning folks who drop the goods into today's slippery plastic probably will never know the beauty of a perfectly packed 20-pound Kraft paper bag.

There is logic in packing a grocery bag. If the order is large, two bags will be required. In a two-bag order, each bag must be balanced in weight for easy carrying. No plastic slits, which cut into the hands, but real arm-holding paper sacks.

To this day, I could pack a good grocery bag with my eyes closed. You squared off the bottom of the paper bag with a box of Rinso, SuperSuds or canned goods. You might then add a package of powder sugar and beside it a bottle of vinegar. Only one bottle to a bag, lest two of them bang against each other and break.

Around this, you nestled some crunchy things, like Independent Baking Co. saltines in a box. Always, at the top for safety's sake, came the eggs. Eggs were taken directly from the crate and carefully nestled into smaller paper bags in this pre-carton period of life.

Now, we came to the true artistry of packing a paper grocery sack. There is no possible art in filling a slippery plastic bag and making it look good. But my papa taught us how to make a certain form of still life in a big brown paper grocery bag.

You always saved the produce for the very top, a basket of fresh strawberries, a head of lettuce. Often, he would throw in a free fresh peach or an apple as a decoration for the top of the bag. And always, and I mean always, the stalk of fresh celery, with its perky green foliage protruding, went in at the top. That foliage made it look like a bouquet arrangement.

"Make the sack something that people will be proud to carry out of our grocery store," he would harp.

Neatly filled squared-off grocery sacks gave my dad a sense of peaceful order. At the time, it seemed like a lot of extra work, but as I see my groceries haphazardly slipped into plastic bags today, I realize we have forfeited something special.

Oh, well ... just drop those groceries into the trunk and get going, or the kids will be late for soccer practice.

❧

The loss of a child is the worst that can happen to a parent. It is worse than the loss of a mate. When our youngest, a witty and talented young guy, died of a brain hemorrhage, we were devastated. We will never recover and, though tragic, it has been within me to write of him, to write the things I needed to say.

To Peter ...

Thanks for being with us for these 36 years

So long, pal, tennis partner and Bix fan ... would-be theatrical hopeful and tenor singer. The cheeriest person I ever knew ... perhaps, would-be newspaper person. You were a good writer, better than I could ever hope to be. And you were simply a grand guy.

So long, Peter my son. You were with us 36 years longer than we ever believed or dreamed possible.

You know, Pete, that you were never expected to live to your 6-month birthday. But you blessedly fooled us all. The neurosurgeons at Children's Memorial Hospital in Chicago were astounded by their success in two landmark marathon surgeries, clamping off an aneurysm that had attached itself to your little brain.

"If he's lucky, he may live to be 5, but we don't know what kind of child he will be," we were warned. They spoke hesitantly of a boy who might — to use a cruel word — be a vegetable.

How can I forget, Peter, the note you wrote to your lead neurosurgeon, Dr. Luis Amador, after you graduated from Bettendorf High:

"I graduated with honors and have been accepted at St. Olaf's; you must have put some fertilizer inside when you were working on my brain."

You were a walking, ticking time bomb, certainly not expected to live past puberty; certainly not to live and love and be married and to have two children. You did, with class.

Well, Peter was found dead Sunday night. He was alone at home, on the bathroom floor in his sleeping clothes. When the call came, "Peter is dead," I spoke to my wife: "It's the aneurysm. I know." We both knew. The autopsy concurred. Death was instantaneous.

There was a bright pumpkin on the porch of the home of Peter and Teri Wundram when we arrived, and my hysterical mind could only hark to the thought that Peter — a mere child of 36 — would be 37 on Halloween. Only days before, he had said, "I don't want a party. I'm too old for parties, but you can make me a marble cake."

Peter was born late on Halloween night. Those were long-ago days when I ran the Halloween Mardi Gras parade, and I forewarned my wife that she could not have the baby until after the parade was over. Dr. E.A. Motto, who helped deliver Peter, christened him at birth. "He's got to be Peter — for Peter, Peter, the pumpkin eater."

For years, at least until he was 5 or 6, Peter would sit on the Halloween parade judges' stand with people like Paul Ives and Shirley Davis and firmly believed that the parade was in his honor ... a birthday parade.

Peter's middle name was Thomas, giving him the coveted initials of P.T. Wundram, which I always claimed was my preference so he could refer to himself as a self-styled circus king, after P.T. Barnum.

Oh, the memories crowd, so poignant. How, after our wives had gone to sleep, Peter and I would sneak away, meet up and go to hear the last set each night at the Bix Jazz Fest ... the touch football on the front lawn ... the snowman elephant we made ... the model train layout we intended to make, but never did. And your love of basketball: This Saturday, you would have coached your first game of the season in a Family Y league.

Peter was a glad-hander, a trait he may have inherited, and he found himself a self-styled singer with a quartet of doctors who called themselves the Second Opinion. They had a gig to sing Sunday night. They couldn't find Peter. He didn't answer the phone. He was dead.

The most difficult thing I will ever do in my life was to kneel on the floor and, sobbing out of control, kiss his lovely, lean cheek.

John F. Kennedy said when his son, Patrick, died: "Parents are not supposed to live longer than their children."

Weeping, weeping, weeping, I say the most tragic thing in a parent's life is to lose a child.

So long, Peter. We love you.

❧

A pumpkin for Peter

I will carve a pumpkin for Peter. For 36 years, I have carved a pumpkin for our son, Peter Wundram. He was born on Halloween, and even when he grew to manhood, I always carved a pumpkin for him. We always laughed, as if neither of us ever quite grew up.

This year, though, after carving the pumpkin, I will place it beside his gravestone at Oakdale Memorial Park.

Peter died a year ago of a massive brain hemorrhage. He was 36, and on his gravestone a pumpkin is engraved, and so I feel it suitable to put a pumpkin beside him — though it will be a sad-faced pumpkin.

I shall never forget, at his moment of birth on a Halloween night, that our friend, Dr. E.A. Motto, beamed: "It's a boy, a boy, and he shall be named Peter — for Peter, Peter, the pumpkin eater."

No one can understand the pain of parents who lose a child except other parents who have lost a child. Well-meaning people have spoken to us of ultimate closure, but that word closure is vague, and I never understood what it meant.

I was numb when Peter died. I cried a lot, and I still do. Life is supposed to mean all that it was ever meant to be, but it doesn't.

Peter, I want to call you by your familiar name, "Pete," and to speak to you in your easy, happy way. I want to call you at night, and say, "Let's go down to the Bix and hear the last set." I want to reminisce about the last time we were on the stage together in a Junior League Follies. I want you to be in the row with us at Open Cities, when all of us — Julia and Diane and Greg and pals from the paper — would take a shopping bag of popcorn and laugh ourselves silly at the Marx Brothers.

I want to laugh, as we always laughed together. You are out of sight, but not out of our minds.

Hemingway wrote, "Life breaks everyone, but the tough become strong in the broken places." Peter's mom and I have not become stronger; we have grown weaker.

Tonight, my wife and I will read anew letters we received in the year since your death. Like your dad, you had the same complex that neither of us ever amounted to much in this vast scheme of life. But you *did* amount to very much to many people. We will reread letters that showed your fun for life, like the one from a high school friend, reciting The Gospel According to Peter: "That you can always find enough change on the floor of a car to buy a package of Ding Dongs; that old cars, like your Betsy and Oscar are best; that baked potatoes taste best when roasted under a pile of burning leaves."

I will reread the long letter from your young German teacher, new at the game and expecting that every one of her students should master German.

After a disastrous test, she said: " 'Peter, you are from German relatives; I cannot understand why you cannot master the language.' I shall never forget his response. With a twinkle in his eye and his inevitable grin, he replied without missing a beat, 'Frau Brown-Lowe, have you ever met any of my relatives?' It was one of the best lines I ever heard, and it endeared me to Peter forever. He became a star in other fields, and it taught me — a just-beginning teacher — that all students have different talents and strengths. I am but one such lucky soul to have learned from him."

Heartening are the letters I received from unknowns, people who say they are "just a reader." You are not "just a reader," but in my sentimental way, you are my family.

One of his friends wrote, "By now, Peter is singing his favorite songs with Frank (Sinatra) and rushing to the TV to watch 'Jeopardy.'" Dave, a childhood friend and owner of a major company, wrote, "Peter's compassion and kindness are the foundation for the man I am today."

I shall not go on, but this is within me, and I must write. I just wanted to say, one more time:

"So long, Pete. We love you."

❧

62 steps to a star

A clear, crisp night with a red glow around us, in search of a star named Peter

It was 6:30 p.m., chilly, a November night with the heavens above Rock Island so brightly sprinkled with stars that I was assured God himself had done the scattering. The moon was brilliant. I could see the man in it and imagined where Neil Armstrong had planted the American flag.

"I have done the computations. Computers helped. The night is so clear; autumn is best for things like this. I think — well, honestly I know — we will be able to spot your star," said Mel Peterson, retired and astronomer laureate at John Deere Planetarium on the campus of Augustana College.

He met us at the bright ground-level doorway, leading up exactly 62 steps to the planetarium's 100-power telescope. The climb was steep, up a winding, concrete stairway as in a castle's round donjon. At the top we gathered in a circular chamber, dimly lit by a small red lamp. It was like a photo darkroom. In the center was that 14-inch reflector telescope, with a spidery guidance contraption that looked like something for a lunar landing.

Months earlier we had met Mel at a party, casually mentioning that some wonderful friends had purchased a star in the heavens and named it for our late son, Peter Thomas Wundram. Such things are possible through the International Star Registry in Switzerland. We hinted that perhaps Mel, during some idling nights, might be able to locate the star, and when visible, share a look at it through the Deere telescope.

Always the eager scientist, Mel accepted the challenge. "Provide me the coordinates, I'll search," he promised.

Along with its registry, we had received a complicated fold-out, coffee table size map directing us to Peter the Star, among billions, in the Milky Way. Circled was a minuscule red dot which showed Peter, a pinpoint in the galaxy.

Mel had done a bunch of calculating; he came up with a handful of other charts showing that Peter would be in the Constellation Draco, known to earthlings like us as "The Dragon." In the official star registry, it would be computed in the region of "GSC 3535:1930." This, of course, meant nothing to an ignoramus like me. I could only imagine Peter chuckling over our personal befuddlement.

Mel pushed buttons to sweep open the giant dome, groaning on its own track, making us even closer to the stars. He fussed in the dim, eerie light, pointing a pencil-thin index finger over more charts, and then pushing keys and buttons on a computer.

"A perfect night. This time of the year is right. Perfect," Mel repeated. He had "Peter" fully programmed for a rendezvous with his parents. The telescope made eerie "Star Wars" squeaks as it cautiously raised and lowered into position.

First, as our warmup to the heavens, Mel focused on Jupiter, which is 11 times bigger than earth. We saw a wide center band and convinced ourselves that we spotted a nearby red ellipse, a giant storm. This was an awesome encounter, to be so close to the heavens, for on this night the moon seemed close enough to touch, and we felt obliged to speak only in whispers. Mel joked that we now could be convinced that it was not made of green cheese.

"It's time to get to the business at hand," he said confidently. "Don't expect too much; the 'Star Peter' we're aiming for is not bright, never visible to the naked eye."

On the third step of a ladder, he peered into the telescope's eyepiece. In the dim of the soft red light, I sensed his satisfying sigh: "I've got it." Then, in the manner of Ed McMahon calling Johnny Carson, he said: "And here-e-e-e's Peter."

My wife and I climbed the ladder, to peer long and hard into the eyepiece.

At 6:50 p.m., in a galaxy far, far away, was a dim little star named Peter Thomas Wundram.

It was a moment of closure.

&❧

-30-